UNFILTERED

www.penguin.co.uk

Also by Guenther Steiner

SURVIVING TO DRIVE

UNFILTERED

MY INCREDIBLE DECADE IN FORMULA 1

GUENTHER STEINER

bantam

TRANSWORLD PUBLISHERS
Penguin Random House, One Embassy Gardens,
8 Viaduct Gardens, London SW11 7BW
www.penguin.co.uk

Transworld is part of the Penguin Random House group of companies
whose addresses can be found at global.penguinrandomhouse.com

First published in Great Britain in 2024 by Bantam
an imprint of Transworld Publishers

Copyright © Guenther Steiner 2024

Guenther Steiner has asserted his right under the Copyright,
Designs and Patents Act 1988 to be identified as the author of this work.

Every effort has been made to obtain the necessary permissions with
reference to copyright material, both illustrative and quoted. We apologize
for any omissions in this respect and will be pleased to make the
appropriate acknowledgements in any future edition.

A CIP catalogue record for this book
is available from the British Library.

ISBNs
9780857506238 hb
9780857506245 tpb

Text design by Couper Street Type Co.
Typeset in 12/17.5 pt Bembo MT Pro by Jouve (UK), Milton Keynes
Printed and bound in Great Britain by Clays Ltd, Elcograf S.p.A.

The authorized representative in the EEA is Penguin Random House Ireland,
Morrison Chambers, 32 Nassau Street, Dublin D02 YH68.

No part of this book may be used or reproduced in any manner for the purpose of
training artificial intelligence technologies or systems. In accordance with Article 4(3)
of the DSM Directive 2019/790, Penguin Random House expressly
reserves this work from the text and data mining exception.

Penguin Random House is committed to a sustainable
future for our business, our readers and our planet. This book is
made from Forest Stewardship Council® certified paper.

*For my family and for all the guys at
Haas F1 past and present.*★

★*Except you, Gene!!*

CONTENTS

Foreword by Toto Wolff ix
Introduction 1

2009–2015
The Idea 7
The Money. 16
The Licence 27
The Recruitment Drive 38
The Drivers 50

2016
The Test. 59
The First Two Races 70
The Learning Curve 81

2017
The Changes 93
The Season 102

2018
The Calm Before the Storm. 123
The Storm 129
The Best Yet. 134
The Beans 140
The Disqualification 146

2019
The Title Sponsor 163
The Season 169

2020
The Pandemic 179
The Fallout. 185
The Reshuffle. 190
The Restart 195

2021
The Rebuild 213
The Season 220

2022
The Light at the End of the Tunnel 233
The Invasion 238
The Replacement 245
The Viking Comeback 250
The Dilemma 256
The Turnaround 261
The Pole 266

2023
The Overview 279
The Test 285
The Season 286

December 2023
Haasta la Vista, Baby 301

Acknowledgements 317
Picture Acknowledgements 319

FOREWORD BY TOTO WOLFF

I must confess that I was in two minds when Guenther asked me to write this foreword. On the one hand, I was flattered that he would consider me for the job. On the other, I had to ask myself: does the world really need another f★★★ing Guenther book?!

Guenther's passport says he is Italian, but during his time in F1 he has always been 'einer von uns' in the sport's Austrian gang. From Niki to Helmut (Marko), to Franz (Tost) and Guenther – all of them direct, pragmatic and opinionated.

No doubt, Austrians are over-represented in Formula 1 and our landscape shapes our character. We generally have two kinds of people: those who grow up with the right level of oxygen in the air, and people from the mountains. Guenther is one of the latter – and maybe that explains a few things. He and I are both university dropouts, and we've had to learn on our feet: maybe that's a reason we've always got on so well.

During his time with Haas, Guenther developed what we can politely call a 'unique' leadership style. It was like he read a management textbook, then decided to do the opposite in almost every situation. Hearing some of the stories of his people management, it's as if this butcher's son simply continued the family business. But as is often the case when you ignore the textbooks, it somehow worked.

He had a vision for a team and found with Gene an entrepreneur who shared and funded that vision. He cleverly maximized the F1 rules to partner with established players to deliver the car. He built a team that could outperform its resources with strong qualifying and race performances. And finally, the way he stands out from the crowd made him gold dust for the filmmakers at Netflix – well, that and his potty mouth.

Guenther's story is about hard work, ingenuity and determination; from rallying, through US motorsport to his time in F1, first as a team boss and now as a pundit with RTL.

I like to think that in his latest role, he's picked up the baton from Niki, and that he will bring his own unique and uncompromising take on the sport.

But I'm sure, too, that his adventures at the sharp end of Formula 1 are not over yet . . .

Toto Wolff
Brackley, UK
June 2024

INTRODUCTION

OK, my friends, this is it. The beginning of the very end of an era. An era that lasted over a decade and saw me, an old Italian man from the mountains where the air is thin called Guenther who speaks German as his first language and Italian as his second yet has dual American citizenship and who lives in North Carolina (I know, I'm some kind of foking weirdo), set up a Formula 1 team from scratch with the help of a Californian machine tool manufacturer and a prancing horse and in the process raised more than a few eyebrows, pissed off one hell of a lot of people (but only the right people, I think), finished sixth in our very first race which surprised a hell of a lot of people, then finished fifth in the Constructors' Championship, and last in the Constructors' Championship (possibly more than once, I forget), found some excellent sponsors (and some not so excellent sponsors), declared war on the FIA on an almost weekly basis, had my doors fok smashed in by an angry Danish pixie, watched an even madder Frenchman crash into a barrier at 145mph and in the process singe the fok out of his hands but live to tell the tale (thank God), achieved a pole position, created more drama than every Italian opera combined, had a hell of a lot of fun, covered about a million miles flying around the globe, met literally thousands of amazing people (as well as one or two wankers), inadvertently 'entertained' a few people on TV by having no filter and by not giving a shit what people think about me, and was unceremoniously relieved of my professional services while shopping for ham in a supermarket.

How's that for setting the scene? Seriously, guys, are you ready for this? It's going to be a rollercoaster.

To set the record straight, I actually spent twelve years in Formula 1, not ten, so the subtitle of this book is a load of bullshit. Then again, I am not going to be talking so much about my two years with Niki Lauda at Jaguar, apart from the odd story here and there, so that should prevent any assholes from trying to sue me.

While I'm on the subject of Jaguar though, do you know who one of the first people was to message me after Haas released their statement about letting me go? Eddie Irvine. What, you've never heard of him? Perhaps I should explain. Eddie was a racing driver back in the olden days and drove for me and Niki at Jaguar when we couldn't get anybody better. Ring any bells? Eddie makes the young Fernando Alonso look like the Pope when it comes to his ego. He called me up a little while ago moaning about the fact that I didn't mention him much in my last book, *Surviving to Drive*.

'I'll make sure I get you in the next one,' I said to him.

'Do you promise, Guenther?' he replied. 'It means a lot to me.'

'I promise. You just leave it to me. I'll make sure you have at least two paragraphs all to yourself.'

As well as being the only driver I have ever achieved a podium with (so far), Eddie is an international playboy who is literally shitting money and in my experience it's always wise to keep in with those people. Incidentally, shortly before the Italian Grand Prix in 2023 I was interviewed by Sky Sports UK and for some reason the podium Eddie had while I was at Jaguar, which to this day is one of the biggest shocks I've had in my life as the car was completely shit, came up in conversation. A few minutes later I received a WhatsApp message from Eddie and when I opened it there was a photo of his old Mitsubishi Shogun. 'I'll have a podium before you and I'm driving this shit heap,' it said. Harsh, but fair.

Anyway, let's get back to what you are about to read.

When Gene Haas first informed me that he did not want to renew my contract, the full details of which you will read about towards the end of this book, one of the first things that occurred to me was that now it had all come to an end I should get it down on paper. I'd already been asked to write a sequel to *Surviving to Drive* but to be honest I'd been short on ideas, and then this happened.

That night I lay in bed thinking about it and over two or three hours I relived the entire story. Having the initial idea about starting a competitive F1 team on a small budget – an American team, that is – contacting Stefano Domenicali who was then at Ferrari and who was the first person to suggest that it might be possible for us to become a customer team to the prancing horse, then talking to Gene about financing it, then to Bernie Ecclestone, Charlie Whiting and the FIA about supporting it and giving us a licence, then getting the foking licence, then putting the infrastructure in place and recruiting the team, then building the car, then recruiting the drivers, then turning up to test for the first time, then turning up to race for the first time, and then trying my best to keep the whole damn thing afloat. I never thought for a moment that I wouldn't be able to do it, but then I never thought that I would, either. I just put my head down, got on with it all and did my best.

This probably isn't the final time you'll either read or hear me say this in this book, but in the last ten years I have lived and breathed Formula 1 twenty-four hours a day, seven days a week, 365 days a year, and from the position of somebody who set up a team from scratch and made it viable. There are very few of us left these days. Jackie Stewart, Ron Dennis and Eddie Jordan are the only guys I can think of. Is it only us now?

Whatever you might think about me or about what has taken place over the past ten years, everyone who has been involved in Haas F1 has an awful lot to be proud of. We also have a story to tell. A story that involves laughter, tears, success, failure, quite a bit of bullshit, shock, amazement, irritation, good decisions, bad decisions, foking awful decisions, anger, tragedy, stupidity, revelations and the occasional bit of industrial bad language. Isn't that what everyone wants from a book these days? I hope so, because it's what you're about to get. And I promise, after this, no more lists!

I hope you enjoy the ride.

Guenther Steiner
North Carolina
Spring 2024

2009-2015

THE IDEA

Over the past few days I've been trying to remember the exact point in time when the idea of starting a Formula 1 team occurred to me and then when I finally made the decision to put the wheels in motion and try my luck. It's all so long ago now and my memory's a bit shit. You know the history though, right, involving the whole USF1 disaster? OK, just in case you are not aware of this, I will tell you.

In early 2009, two men, the journalist Peter Windsor, who had also worked for Ferrari and Williams, and Ken Anderson, who ironically had once been the technical director at the NASCAR team that Gene Haas co-owns with Tony Stewart, Stewart-Haas Racing, announced to the world their intention to launch an American Formula 1 team – the first since 1986 – which would also be the only F1 team based outside Europe. I remember it was very big news at the time, but what I also remember is that very few people in the sport thought it would ever be a success. Formula 1 was still a minority sport in the States, despite the fact that the general public loved their motorsport: the likes of NASCAR and IndyCar were beloved, very popular and had been part of the sporting fabric of the country for decades. What chance did F1 stand?

What isn't commonly known is that the first Grand Prix in the US actually took place in 1908, some forty-two years before the inaugural F1 World Championship. The race was won, incidentally, by the Frenchman Louis Wagner, who went on to win the first official British Grand Prix in 1926. This information did not come from my own memory, by the way. Fortunately, as you'd expect for a sport obsessed with data, every fragment of F1's history has been well recorded.

For F1 in the United States, the hundred or so years that followed that first race were eventful to say the least, although usually not in a good way, and reached absolute rock bottom in 2005 when, due to some tyre concerns, just six cars lined up on the grid for the US Grand Prix. The crowd started booing, I remember, and I switched off my TV set when it was all done and said to my wife Gertie something along the lines of, 'Wow, what a shit show!' Subsequently, the sport's reputation in the US, which was already on dodgy ground, took an absolute foking hammering and two years later F1 left America altogether.

An attempt to rehabilitate the sport in the US wasn't made until 2010 when the city of Austin in Texas was awarded a ten-year deal to host the US Grand Prix from 2012 onwards at a brand-new purpose-built circuit. So when Peter and Ken announced their intention to start an American F1 team at the beginning of 2009, the reputation of the sport was still in tatters. Even so, a few months later they were granted a licence from Bernie and the FIA and with that entry to the 2010 Formula 1 World Championship. What could possibly go wrong?

One of the reasons I know a little bit about this is because USF1's factory and headquarters had been set up in Charlotte,

THE IDEA

North Carolina, which is close to where I'd already been living for several years. Moreover, I had recently started a composite company called Fibreworks with a friend of mine, which he runs and we co-own to this day, and we'd been approached by USF1 about doing some design work for them and supplying some parts. At the very start of that relationship I was quite excited because I had no idea where it might lead. After a few weeks, though, it became clear to me that everything was not as it should be. Put simply, nobody at the team's factory seemed to know what the hell they were doing, and I feared the worst.

Word eventually got out about our relationship with the USF1 Team and I reluctantly became one of the go-to people when the interested parties at F1 – Bernie Ecclestone, race director Charlie Whiting, etc. – wanted to know how the team were progressing. Not that I could tell them a great deal, at least at first. Bernie was the first person to contact me. 'Hey, Guenther, I'm worried that they won't be ready in time,' he said to me. 'Could you keep your ear to the ground?' Of course, I told him, and over the coming weeks I kept a close eye on things (or as close as I could get) and made a few enquiries. The idea of having a new F1 team based in the US obviously appealed to Bernie and the guys at F1, but the distances involved made it difficult for them to police things, monitor progress and ensure they could produce a viable racing outfit.

It didn't take me long to find out that the team were in big trouble, which came as no great surprise, and the general consensus was that they wouldn't be ready in time for the 2011 season, let alone 2010, which was the target.

'They haven't got a foking clue,' I remember saying to Bernie.

'OK,' he said. 'I'd better send somebody out.'

I think Bernie's representative arrived in Charlotte in December 2009, and although he never told me what they found, Charlie Whiting visited the site a couple of months later. Soon after that they decided to pull the plug which brought an end to the shit show. It was never going to work and by allowing it to carry on it would have damaged the sport. Somebody could write a book about the USF1 debacle. The guys meant well, I'm sure, but they were completely out of their depth.

While all of this was unfolding I had been asking myself whether an American F1 team might just be feasible, if it was done properly. By the time USF1 folded I still hadn't made up my mind about this but I decided to carry on investigating. I don't think the Austin deal had been announced by this point but I figured that the idea was still worth exploring. I was in no rush though.

Then, a few weeks after the USF1 Team fell apart, I received a telephone call out of the blue from a guy called Chad Hurley. Chad, who was one of the co-inventors of YouTube and had recently sold it to Facebook for a boatload of foking money, had been one of the main investors in USF1 and wanted to know if, in my opinion, there was any way of him being able to get a car on the grid for the following season. At the time, I was probably one of the only people based in the United States who had some knowledge of how Formula 1 worked so I said I'd have a think about it and make a few telephone calls.

'The only option you have,' I said to Chad a few days later, 'is to explore the idea of buying the two HRT cars.'

The Madrid-based HRT Team were in big financial trouble at

the time and hadn't been able to pay the €7 million they owed a company called Dallara, who had been building their cars.

'As far as I know the cars are at a pretty advanced stage,' I told Chad. 'So why not fly over there and see if you can do a deal?'

'But I don't know them,' said Chad. 'Could you go for me? You already said that you know the owner of Dallara.'

I'm not sure what made me do it, but I ended up agreeing to Chad's request and caught the next flight out to Parma in Italy, which is close to the Dallara factory. I had known the founder and owner of Dallara, Mr Giampaolo Dallara, for several years and when I put the idea to him he was responsive. There were issues though, such as whether Dallara actually owned the cars in the first place. Also, regardless of whether they did or not, it was going to take a lot more than just buying a couple of cars to get on the starting grid. It was time to call another of my contacts.

Stefano Domenicali, who is now the CEO of the Formula One Group but whose career highlight so far is writing the introduction to my first book, *Surviving to Drive*, had been the team principal of Scuderia Ferrari since 2008 and we'd been friends since my days at Jaguar. As I was in Italy I decided to pay him a visit, partly because I wanted his opinion on the cars and the HRT situation, but also because the food at the Ferrari factory at Maranello is amazing and I wanted a free lunch. 'Don't have anything to do with it, Guenther,' Stefano advised. 'You won't get it through. The whole thing is a poisoned chalice. You have a good reputation in Formula 1, don't ruin it.'

As much as I trusted and valued Stefano's opinion (especially about my reputation in Formula 1) I decided to call Bernie, just in case I was missing something from the very top. After all, Formula 1 was still his property and if anyone could give me the final word on it all, he could. I ended up having two meetings with Bernie. Not because we were making progress, but because the whole thing was so ridiculously complicated.

'It's too foking messy,' I said to Chad. 'I'm sorry, but it's time to call it a day.'

Naturally he was disappointed as he'd wasted millions of dollars, but there was nothing more I could do.

Apart from a free trip to Italy, some interesting conversations and a nice lunch, the one thing I came away with from that process was the realization that, given my experience and contacts, should I ever wish to do so, I could probably have a good go at putting a Formula 1 team together myself. By now the Austin agreement had been announced, which made the idea of having an American team both feasible and attractive. What scared me though was the amount of money that would have to be invested in infrastructure. This had been the undoing of several teams already (more would go later on) and was one of several reasons why the sport was in crisis. If memory serves me correctly there was even a possibility that there might not be enough cars on the grid in 2011 and 2012.

This forced Bernie and the FIA to start looking at ways in which interested parties might be able to mitigate some of the upfront and ongoing costs that were associated with starting, running and in some cases ruining a Formula 1 team. One of the most viable and attractive ideas, in my opinion, was to allow new teams to buy transferable parts from existing manufacturers in order to keep costs down. On one level it solved

THE IDEA

the sustainability issue, but at the same time it also provided income for manufacturers.

Although I liked the idea, I wanted to see if there was some way we could make the whole thing relationship-driven (between the new and existing team) as opposed to just transactional. Not a partnership, exactly, more of a collaboration. I then decided to phone Charlie Whiting.

'Under the new rules,' I began, 'if I started a team, what could and couldn't I buy from a manufacturer?'

'Everything apart from the chassis,' he said. 'And you obviously have to do your own aerodynamics.'

'So, I could form a relationship with a team whereby we became a customer of theirs yet were able to develop our own technology and potentially even learn from each other?'

'Well, there's nothing in the current rules that says you can't do that,' said Charlie.

Despite what Charlie said, I was doubtful. I had no idea whether a manufacturer might go for something like that. The customer team idea had already ruffled more than a few feathers in the sport (especially the smaller teams that were struggling financially) so taking it to another level might be too much. 'Don't be stupid, Guenther,' said my old boss Niki Lauda when I told him. He was working for Mercedes at the time and was a perfect sounding board. 'Providing there are parameters in place,' he said, 'why shouldn't it work? After all, everyone benefits.'

'And what about Bernie?'

'You leave Bernie to me,' said Niki. 'If and when the time comes, I will speak with him.'

The first manufacturer I met with was Mercedes. Although they were cautiously enthusiastic about the idea, when it came to cost they were just too expensive. With hindsight, I'm actually glad that this was the case as by far the most natural fit, for me both as an Italian and as a potential team principal, was Ferrari. That might sound a bit egotistical, but at the end of the day I was the only person working on this idea so I had to start with me. Also, not only was Stefano Domenicali a good friend of mine, but I also had quite a few friends who worked at the Ferrari factory in Maranello. It felt like the right approach.

Just as I'd done with Mercedes, I had several meetings with Stefano and his colleagues at Ferrari. This time, though, there was no caution in their enthusiasm. 'I like the idea,' said Stefano. 'So, if you find the money, we'll try and make it work.'

Although I have just referred to myself as a team principal, or at least a potential team principal, I actually had no idea what my role might consist of (in detail, at least) if my idea ever came to fruition. After all, team principals were usually hired by the teams or manufacturers, whereas I was trying to start a team from scratch and find a manufacturer to work with. Also, having run the Jaguar Team alongside Niki Lauda, I knew exactly what the traditional team principal role entailed. My role probably would be much wider, but that's all I knew at the time.

While I wasn't reinventing the wheel exactly, there was no blueprint in place for what I was doing or what I had in mind – or at least not one that had either been executed recently or had succeeded. That's part of what made it exciting. Had I simply been copying someone else's formula, it wouldn't have appealed to me as much so I probably wouldn't have done it. Formula 1 is all about progression via innovation, and in my own very small way that's exactly what I was doing.

'What's the next step?' Gertie asked when I returned from Maranello.

'The next step is the money,' I said. 'I need to find a multi-millionaire.'

THE MONEY

These days Formula 1 is probably one of the richest sports on the planet. Even smaller teams like Haas have been valued at around $1 billion recently and so the future of the sport has never looked brighter, at least financially. Back in 2011, which is when I started looking for investment, things were very different. For a start, it was a much smaller sport, both in terms of its global popularity and the number of people who were involved. Financially, it was like chalk and cheese.

Apart from now being a sport for billionaires as opposed to millionaires, F1 is seen as being a safe bet investment-wise, and interested parties are literally clamouring to get on the grid. Why? Because it's more popular than it's ever been and is run equitably — or at least a hell of a lot more equitably than it was in 2011. The concept of becoming a customer team did nothing to mitigate the inequality that existed between the teams in those days — if anything, it reinforced it — but that didn't put me off. Bernie couldn't cling on for ever, and once he'd gone, who knows, things might change.

The first thing I did once I had decided to look for investment was put together a business plan. I still have this in my possession and including the cover it's just eight pages long. The reason for this is that it existed more as a talking point than a document detailing the idea. I can certainly do detail if I have to, but I much prefer to provide it *after* an initial conversation has taken place. When I first started talking to Gene Haas, for instance, he asked me questions almost constantly and that carried on until long after we got the licence.

This also demonstrates one of the major differences between how we did things then (or should I say, how I did things) and how you would have to do them these days, which once again is representative of how the sport has changed. I cannot think of any scenario today within F1 where somebody could turn up with an eight-page printed PowerPoint proposal and do business, least of all start a brand-new team. It was something that I had to get my head around very quickly, and as the sport changed I was happy to adapt. I might be old and decrepit but I'm not completely stupid.

Between 2011 and 2013 I must have met with five or six people about investing in the team, so not many. There was plenty of positivity, at least initially, but none of the interested parties came anywhere near to saying yes. I cannot say for sure what that was down to. It could have been me, the proposal, the state of the sport at the time, or all three. I wasn't too disappointed though. After all, this was what my friends in the rally garages in the UK used to call 'a punt'. Sure, I thought the idea could work, but I also knew that the chances of raising the money were slim. Looking back, had I not had the contacts I had in the sport, I don't think I would have lasted too long. In fact, I would go so far as to say that it was their influence and encouragement that kept me going, in particular Stefano, Niki and Charlie.

What I should explain here is that, until a certain point in time which I will come to in a few pages, this was never my motivation for getting out of bed in the morning. Fok, no. It sounds a bit crazy when you read it on paper, but to me, starting a Formula 1 team was just a part-time hobby with a big fat dream tied to the end of it. My company, Fibreworks, had started in 2009 and the majority of my time since then had been spent helping to build it up. That was my bread and butter, although for the first few years there wasn't much of either. That said, it had always been a dream of mine to start a company, either on my own or with a partner, and I loved every moment of it.

Someone else who encouraged me to carry on pursuing the idea of starting an F1 team was Gertie. For the majority of the time we had been together I had been involved in motorsport in some shape or form and she knew that deep down I was keen to get back to it. Every so often she would ask me if there was any news and would share in my excitement if, for instance, I had found a potential investor. Conversely, she would also commiserate when it all went tits up, which it obviously did every time until I found Gene.

With hindsight, it was important for me to have a sounding board outside F1, as if I hadn't it would have become too much of an echo chamber. Stefano, Niki and Charlie were all great, but they were also totally engrained in the sport. I needed a kind of leveller, and Gertie was perfect. She also made very good suggestions sometimes, such as giving the team a name.

'What do you mean, give it a name?' I said when she first suggested this.

'When you make your presentation,' said Gertie. 'You can't just call it "Guenther Steiner's Formula 1 Team".'

She had a point. If somebody was astute and intelligent enough to give Guenther Steiner tens of millions of dollars to spend on a shiny new Formula 1 team they would undoubtedly want to have a say in this; the team needed to have a name.

'That's a really good point,' I said. 'Let me have a think about it.'

I was conscious not to include my own name in the title and so after doing some research I settled on the North American Racing Team, or NART. This name had been used before in motorsport by a man called Luigi Chinetti. From the late 1950s until the late 1960s this Italian-born émigré to the US raced primarily in endurance racing, with a great deal of success. He also raced in F1, in which he also did well, but only in North America and Mexico.

By far the most striking similarity between Luigi's NART and the one I was proposing was that each of us had relied (or would be reliant) on a relationship with Ferrari. The reason Luigi started NART back in 1958 was to promote the Ferrari marque in North America. He'd been selling Ferraris by the truckload in the territory for years and when he came up with the idea of racing them (in endurance racing first) Ferrari agreed to provide cars, factory mechanics and as much support as he needed.

Adhering to the widely held view that Ferrari made some of the best cars in the world, NART only entered cars in the most prestigious races, such as 24 Hours of Le Mans, 12 Hours of Sebring and 24 Hours of Daytona, and had victories in all three. Despite the fact that in Formula 1 they only ever raced in Mexico and North America, in 1964, after entering a Ferrari 158 on behalf of Ferrari's Scuderia works team but under the name of NART, they helped to seal wins for both the Scuderia, who won the International Cup for F1 Manufacturers, and for John Surtees, who won his first and only World Championship. Anyway, after reading all about Luigi's racing team and their relationship with Ferrari, it made sense to follow suit and pay tribute to their endeavours and achievements.

Forza NART!

I cannot name names here, but some time in late 2011 I had a meeting booked in with a potential investor who I genuinely thought might be up for putting his hand in his pocket. He'd been an acquaintance of mine for some time and a certain amount of pre-qualification had already taken place over the phone. Not just by him, but by me too. There were a heck of a lot of time wasters hanging around on the fringes of F1 in those days and I had already had my fingers burned. Or should I say, I had wasted half a day of my foking life on somebody who had no intention of investing but who just wanted to know more about the idea. What a prick!

The meeting with the potential investor (not the prick) went very well indeed and it was the first time I remember thinking that it might actually happen. I'm usually quite good at gauging reactions from people and his was incredibly positive. He also asked what I considered to be all the right questions and didn't seem fazed by the answers – or should I say, by the figures.

'How did it go?' asked Gertie when I arrived home. 'Quite well, by the look on your face.'

'I can't say for sure,' I said, 'but I think I might be on to something. This guy really knows his stuff.'
'Is he rich though?'
'Rich? He's literally shitting foking dollars.'
'GUENTHER!'
'Sorry.'

Did I tell you that I am not supposed to swear when I'm at home? It's true. Gertie's quite strict, and it has something to do with us having a young daughter. I try my best to be good but f-bombs still appear from time to time. What can I say? I spent ten years working in rally and as a consequence I have a mouth like an open sewer sometimes.

About a week later I received a telephone call from the potential investor saying that he was no longer interested. 'It isn't you,' he said, 'or the proposal. It's the sport itself. It's just too volatile and unequitable for my liking. I'm sorry, Guenther.'

'Don't be,' I said. 'I completely understand.'

For a few seconds I was disappointed, but then the unstoppable Steiner optimism began to win through. OK, so he hadn't invested. Neither had anybody else! What he had done was show a genuine interest. He'd thought the proposal was both solid and realistic. Or at least, that's what he said to me. He could have been full of shit for all I know.

'How's it going, Guenther?' Niki asked me over the phone later that day. 'Have you any news at all?'

'I had a really good meeting with a guy last week.'

'Will he invest though?'

'No, but he liked the proposal.'

'He's obviously a foking idiot.'

'Thank you, Niki. I appreciate your support and kind words.'

'No problem, Guenther.'

Because potential investors only seemed to come around every so often I wasn't expecting another one any time soon, but just a week or so after Niki referred to the last one as a foking idiot, a new one materialized, although at the time I didn't realize it.

I was on my way to a meeting in Charlotte when suddenly I saw a familiar face.

'Foking hell, Joe, how are you? I haven't seen you in years.'

I'd known Joe Custer, who ran the Stewart-Haas Racing NASCAR team, since 2005, which is when I moved to North Carolina in order to set up a NASCAR team for Red Bull. For a variety of reasons that hadn't worked out, or at least for me, and I hadn't seen Joe since leaving the team a year later. We chatted for almost an hour, but when I arrived home later that evening I felt uneasy about something. 'Oh, shit!' I said out loud. 'He'd have been perfect!' Fortunately Gertie wasn't in at the time, but what had made me say it was that the owner of Joe's team, Gene Haas, was exactly the kind of person I should be speaking to about the proposal.

'Do you think Mr Haas might be interested?' I asked Joe when I called him about it the following day.

'He could be,' he said. 'But Gene's based in LA. Why don't we meet for a coffee? You can do the presentation for me and if I think Gene might go for it, I'll pass it on to him.'

'Perfect.'

We arranged to meet in my local Starbucks in Mooresville a few days later, and I did the presentation.

'OK, what do you think?' I said after finishing.

'That's pretty interesting,' said Joe.

'Interesting enough to pass on to Mr Haas?'

'I think so,' he said, taking the presentation. 'Gene's in town later this week. Let me give this to him and I'll get back to you as soon as I can.'

I tried my absolute best not to get excited about this but it was foking well impossible. I knew that Gene Haas was based in LA, but he owned a NASCAR team that was based just down the road. Better still, he understood how the motorsport industry worked.

For the next four weeks I didn't hear a peep out of Joe, but that was OK. If Gene had said no he would have told me, so I figured that no news was good news. Then, one Thursday night just after I arrived home, my phone started ringing. It was Joe.

'Hey, Guenther. Gene's in town for the NASCAR race in Charlotte this weekend and he'd like to meet you. Are you free for dinner on Saturday?'

'Too foking right I am!'

So far, every potential investor had been different, in that some of them had been responsive to the presentation and some less so. With Gene it was different again, in that he said almost nothing at all during our first couple of meetings yet I never got the feeling that he wasn't interested. He just kept his cards very close to his chest and used his words sparingly.

'How do you think it went?' I asked Joe on the Monday after dinner.

'Difficult to say,' he said. 'I don't know if you noticed, but Gene doesn't give much away.'

'You're not joking!'

'He'd have let me know if he wasn't interested though, which is the main thing.'

Once again, no news was good news.

Two weeks passed, then one morning I got a call on my mobile from a number it didn't recognize. Normally I'd just ignore such a call but I had a feeling it might be Gene.

'Guenther,' said the caller. 'This is Gene Haas.'

What can I say? I'm a foking genius.

'I've got some questions for you,' he said.

I can't remember what the questions were but I was able to answer them there and then. There was no feedback about the presentation, or about the answers I'd just given him. It was just questions – once answered, gone.

Over the next few weeks Gene's calls became more and more frequent, to the point where I started to expect them. As with the very first call I received, all he ever did was ask questions. Some of these related to the presentation, some to Dallara who would be making the chassis and helping us build the car, some to Ferrari, of course, who would be making the majority of the transferable parts, and some related to the sport in general and the people at the top. Nine times out of ten I would be able to answer the questions either immediately or after making a quick telephone call, which seemed to please Gene. I'll say one thing though: he was certainly very thorough.

This went on for over a year, and although I was desperate to know where Gene was at in terms of the idea, I always decided against trying to force his hand.

'You're an idiot, Guenther,' said Niki one day. 'You've been talking to this man for over a year now. What's wrong with him?'

'Nothing, as far as I know. He calls me up, asks me a load of questions, I answer them, and then he goes.'

'Is he actually interested?'

'To be honest, I have no foking idea, Niki. I hope so.'

'I think it's time he either caught a fish or cut the bait, don't you? Ask him where he is.'

'OK, I will.'

Niki was right. I appreciated that Gene had to be sure before making any decisions but I couldn't think of any questions that hadn't already been answered. Also, everyone's patience was starting to wear a bit thin. Stefano, Bernie, Charlie, and Niki of course. Gene was due in Charlotte that weekend so I decided to ask him then.

'What do you think will happen?' Gertie asked me the day before he arrived.

'I honestly don't know. I was told from day one that if he wasn't interested he'd say so, but I'm not sure if I believe that any more. Or perhaps he's just forgotten to tell me.'

Regardless of the lack of movement and clarity with the situation, I'd always tried to convince myself that it wouldn't happen. This had nothing at all to do with pessimism, it was about realism. Formula 1 was still an incredibly precarious sport (especially if you owned a team) and although I had faith in both my proposal and my ability, I could fully understand why any potential investors would want to walk away. Life's about taking chances, but within reason. I knew that I couldn't completely sell this idea to anybody. They had to *want* to do it.

The following day I received a telephone call from Gene. This time he had just one question for me. 'Can you come to my office at the factory later today? I want to talk to you.' I arrived at Gene's office at about 2 p.m. 'I've just got to dial into a board meeting,' he said to me. I offered to leave the room but he told me not to bother. 'I won't be long,' he assured me.

While he was doing that I decided to send some emails and I was part way through writing the second one when Gene said something that caught my attention. 'Oh, by the way,' he said to his board members, 'Guenther and I are going to be applying for a Formula 1 licence.'

This was news to me!

'Are we really?' I said to Gene when he put down the phone. 'We are.'

After three long years of negotiations with a succession of suitors I was finally on my way.

'But before we talk about that,' he said, 'I've got some questions for you.'

Oh, foking hell.

THE LICENCE

'And about time. I was beginning to think that this man was either a time waster or a lunatic.'

'Gene Haas is neither of those things,' I said to Niki, who had called to offer me his congratulations. 'He's just a very astute and very successful businessman who wants to get his ducks in a row.'

'What, and then ask them a lot of questions? Congratulations, Guenther. You're nearly there.'

Although I had obviously thought everything through prior to first writing and then presenting my proposal to various interested parties, I hadn't really considered how things might change in terms of activity if and when we got to this stage. When it finally happened, it's safe to say that it came as a bit of a shock. As opposed to Gene calling me every other day with questions and Niki every other week to see if there was any progress, my phone started ringing off the hook. Word was starting to get out that Gene and I were applying for a licence and people wanted the lowdown. 'Just foking leave me alone,' I said to most of them. 'We've only just started the process of applying for a licence and that's all I can tell you.'

Fortunately, quite a few of the calls were from people who were involved in the application process and who needed information. This was positive as every call was a reminder that we were making progress.

About a week after we announced that we would be applying for a licence I had to go to Europe on Fibreworks business. At about three o'clock in the morning on the second night of my stay my phone started ringing. Still tired from the journey over, I'd fallen asleep at about 9.30 p.m. and it's safe to say that on being woken up I was far from happy. 'Who the foking hell is this?' I muttered, looking at my phone. The number wasn't recognized but I was so desperate to shout at whoever had woken me from what had been a very deep sleep that I answered it.

'Yes, who is it?' I growled. Whoever it was, they were about to get both foking barrels.

'Guenther, it's Niki,' came the reply. 'I'm in India with Bernie and Stefano. They're here with me now and my phone is on loudspeaker so be careful what you say about them. We've spoken about your application and Bernie has some questions for you.'

'Really?' I said, trying to get out of bed and almost falling flat on my ass in the process. 'OK, Bernie, I'm ready for you,' I said. 'Fire away.'

For the next two hours Bernie Ecclestone, with occasional contributions from Niki Lauda, interrogated me about what I had in mind and how I intended to both execute and sustain the project. Fortunately for me, almost every single question had been asked already by Gene so I was able to give a fairly good account of myself.

'That went quite well,' said Niki the following day. 'He likes the idea and, just as importantly, he likes you. I think. A little bit.'

I couldn't have wished for a better start, despite being taken by surprise.

The next person who wanted to interrogate me was Charlie Whiting, who I knew much better than Bernie, and then Jean Todt, who was the president of the FIA. These discussions were all preliminary, by the way. At Niki's behest they'd been encouraged to get to know both me and the proposal prior to the application going live and us making the official presentation. Stefano too had put in a good word with the likes of Bernie and Jean so it was all very encouraging.

My original idea, by the way, had been to start off using parts that were a year old, thus making the costs lower still. 'That's all good and well,' said Gene, 'but how could we ever be competitive? I'd like parity with Ferrari right from the word go.'

In the end we flew out to Italy to meet Stefano in person, together with Mattia Binotto, who headed up the engine department at Ferrari. 'Parity actually works better for us,' said Stefano, 'as we'd only have to make one model of each part.' Instead of leaving it there, Stefano and I expanded the concept, which led to Haas eventually becoming what is known as a satellite team to Ferrari.

These days a concept like that for a new team would be impossible, for the simple reason that the rules are much tighter. I also think that some of the existing teams might have something to say about it! Back then, the number of parts a customer team could buy from a manufacturer hadn't yet been defined in the rules, simply because nobody had thought about doing it. Everything was still open for discussion, and we took full advantage of that. I've said this many times before, but in this situation either a team runs out of money or an investor runs out of enthusiasm and it was my job to try and make sure that Gene Haas had plenty of both.

The point I kept on trying to get through to everybody during the process, whether it be Gene, Bernie, Charlie or Jean, was that the concept benefited everyone. We'd have parts supplied to us with ongoing support by the most experienced and successful manufacturer on the grid, Formula 1 would have a shiny new team with a far less risky business model than the ones that had gone (and were still going) to shit, and Ferrari would get a new customer that could pay its bills on time and that was keen on developing the relationship further – within the rules, of course. It was the proverbial win-win situation, at least in my eyes.

The first thing I had to do in submitting the licence application was to complete something called a call of interest, which basically informed the FIA of our intentions and let them know who was involved. I'm referring to this in the past tense as the process will probably have changed by now. Anyway, providing that was accepted, you could then submit your application. This is where things got serious as in order to do so you had to pay the FIA a non-refundable bond of €150,000. This was to pay for due diligence conducted by the FIA and to expose any bullshitters.

'So, if we don't get the licence, I'm screwed,' said Gene when I informed him.

'I wouldn't say screwed, exactly. Just a tiny bit poorer. Or should I say, a tiny bit less rich. Anyway, we'll get the licence. You'll see.'

Talk about flying by the seat of your pants!

Looking back, the only thing I can think of that could have derailed us at this point was the fact that Gene was a convicted felon. Although it still isn't too widely known, in January 2006 Gene had begun a two-year prison sentence for tax evasion and had been released on probation sixteen months later. I obviously can't say this for sure but I'd hazard a guess that anyone applying for a Formula 1 licence these days who had a criminal record, and for something that had happened quite recently, wouldn't get past first base. When Gene and I applied, however, things were different. The sport was desperate for new teams so it was a case of eyes, ears, mouths and assholes shut.

For the soccer leagues in Britain, such as the English Premier League, they have something called a Fit and Proper Persons test which is designed to prevent unscrupulous and untrustworthy people either owning a professional soccer club or joining the board of a club. The reason this was put into place, I imagine, was because of previous bad experiences. I'm sure it isn't perfect (not all untrustworthy or unscrupulous people have been caught and/or prosecuted) but I assume it's made a difference.

While I'm not sure what Formula 1's exact position was with regard to who they considered to be fit and proper people to own or run a team, Gene's conviction and subsequent prison sentence were barely even mentioned during the process of us applying for a licence. I have two theories as to why this might have been the case. The first is that the people at the top simply did not care and were just desperate for a new team, and the second is that because I was leading the bid and always did most of the talking (and hadn't been to prison) they didn't consider it to be an issue. The second theory is the most likely, in my opinion, but I think the first probably came into play a bit too.

Funnily enough, the only people who mentioned Gene's conviction during the process of us applying for a Formula 1 licence were some friends within the industry who had heard about the application but weren't actually involved. I cannot mention any names again (sorry, but they'd kill me!) but I received at least seven or eight telephone calls. Most of the people assumed that I didn't know about his conviction, and when I told them that I did they were naturally surprised.

'But do Bernie and the FIA know?' one of them asked.

'Of course they do! It's in the public domain. Gene hasn't tried to hide anything, but at the same time he hasn't been shouting about it from the foking rooftops.'

In all the time I worked with Gene Haas we only had one short conversation about his time in jail, and it taught me two things. First, he got very fit while he was there because he worked out every day, and second, he was in charge of the boiler. That's literally it.

Once the due diligence had been completed, in February 2014 we were invited to make a presentation to the board of the FIA explaining, once again, what we had in mind for the team and how we were going to achieve and sustain it. The only person from the FIA who was not present was the president, Jean Todt. Everyone else was. The legal guys, the technical director, the CEO. And Charlie and Bernie, of course.

The only thing that made me slightly nervous prior to Gene, Joe Custer and I travelling to the FIA headquarters at

Geneva in Switzerland (the presentation actually took place in France as the meeting room we used at the FIA was on the other side of the border) was the fact that I hadn't employed the services of a lawyer. This course of action had been recommended to me by at least a dozen people but I'd always dismissed the idea.

'What the fok would I need a lawyer for?' I said to one of them.

'Erm, to answer any legal questions during the presentation? I take it FIA's lawyers are going to be present?'

'Yes, I suppose so. Don't worry, I'll be fine.'

But as we arrived at the FIA, I had a feeling that I might have been a little bit hasty in dismissing the idea. It was too late now though. It was shit or bust.

The other concern that some people had about the presentation, although not me, was the fact that I wouldn't even be using PowerPoint.

'What are you going to use then?' asked a friend of mine.

'A piece of A4 paper with some bullet points on it.'

'A what?'

'A piece of A4 paper with some foking bullet points on it. What, have you gone deaf or something?'

According to my friend (who to be fair had worked in motorsport for a long time so wasn't a complete idiot), regardless of how many contacts I had in the industry or at the FIA, a presentation to get a team licence for the highest class of international racing for open-wheel single-seater formula racing cars in the world perhaps merited more than a piece of A4 paper with some bullet points written on it. I did actually consider doing a PowerPoint presentation, which is what I had originally prepared for pitching the idea to potential investors like Gene, but in the end I decided against it.

'Everything's in my head,' I said to my friend. 'A PowerPoint presentation would just be a distraction, for me and for them.' This might sound absolutely crazy to some people but I stand by it. It's not as if there were going to be a hundred people in the room (there were about ten) and I wanted them all to concentrate fully on whoever was speaking, not on a foking screen. I also had no script, by the way. The bullet points were all I needed to put forward our case and I was confident that between me, Gene and Joe, we'd be able to answer any and all questions. 'No,' I remember insisting to my friend. 'A PowerPoint presentation would be too much of a distraction. I'm just going to freestyle.'

'Really? Good luck!' he said.

The presentation itself is now a bit of a blur. Not because I was nervous or anything. I don't really get nervous. I'm too laid back for that shit. My philosophy is always, whatever will be will be and as long as I've tried my best I'm OK. I suppose this was slightly different in that I'd been working on it for several years, but if it all came to nothing, what could I do? Fok all. I don't have time to worry about things I cannot change. That's for fools.

Although Gene didn't appear to be nervous either, the closer we had got to the day of the presentation the more I think he worried about what might happen if they said no. I was the one who'd put the work in but he was the one who'd had to shell out €150,000.

The reason the presentation is a blur is because it was all so intense and because I hardly stopped talking for over two hours. After explaining the concept via the bullet points and telling them that if they gave us the licence pigs were going to fly and elephants would sing, which took an hour and a half, we then took questions from the panel which, because of my position and what I knew, I had to answer the vast majority of.

Thinking about it, I went into that meeting feeling pretty confident. I'm quite a confident person naturally, and apart from helping to build up Fibreworks I'd worked on little else for over three years.

'How do you think it went?' Gene asked me when it had finished. 'Do you think we'll get the licence?'

'I honestly don't know, Gene,' I replied. 'That's up to the FIA. We've done everything we can though. Let's just wait and see.'

About five minutes later a message came through on my phone. It was from a member of the FIA board, the identity of whom will have to remain a secret for ever. 'Foking hell, Guenther,' it read. 'Nobody can spout shit like you. If you can't get a licence after that performance, nobody can.'

'Actually, Gene,' I said, 'let's just say that I'm quietly confident.'

On Friday 11 April I boarded a plane from Charlotte to LA to attend the 2014 Toyota Grand Prix of Long Beach, which is usually race two or three of the IndyCar Series. The presentation to the FIA had taken place two months previously and I'd been told by Charlie Whiting a few days ago that a decision on the application was imminent.

The flight from Charlotte to LA took about six hours and after collecting my luggage I turned on my phone and made my way to the exit. After eventually coming to life (my phone used to take an age in those days) it informed me that I had thirty-five new emails. In six hours! I was staying with a friend of mine in LA and while I waited for him to pick me up I started going through them. Shit – delete, shit – delete, shit – delete, shit – delete, Charlie Whiting. Foking hell! The subject of the email read something like 'Licence Decision'. So this was definitely it.

Before I opened the email, I reminded myself once again that if the answer was no, the world would not fall apart and my family and I would still be OK.

'Dear Guenther,' it began. 'I am pleased to inform you that your application for a Super Licence has been successful.'

Unlike so many of the other things that I have been desperately trying to remember while writing this book, I can recall exactly how I reacted to the news about the licence. Emotionally it was just incredible – a mixture of excitement, joy, relief and trepidation – whereas physically all I did was grin for about six hours. Seriously, I looked like I was on drugs! I'll tell you another emotion I felt, and that is pride. Gene had made it possible with his money but I had been responsible for both the idea and the execution. It's not often that I blow my own trumpet but on this occasion I'm willing to give it a quick toot.

The first person I called after receiving the email was Gene. As usual, it was hard to tell whether he felt elated, cheated, depressed or angry. I think he was elated though. 'Well done, Guenther,' he said. 'Now the work begins.' I remember thinking, *begins*? I've been working on this for over three foking years! Gene was right though. I knew when I read the email that for at least the foreseeable future I could kiss goodbye to any kind of social life. I had a Formula 1 team to put together.

THE RECRUITMENT DRIVE

'You look pretty happy today,' Gertie said one morning about a week after we got the licence. 'You're beginning to make a habit of this.'

'That's because I am happy,' I replied. 'I'm seeing Gene in half an hour at the factory, then I've got phone calls with Niki and Charlie.'

'What about this time? Those two must be fed up with you by now.'

'If they were, they would tell me, believe me. Both calls are about my list of things that I have to do. It's getting longer by the minute.'

The main topic of conversation between me, Gene and the FIA immediately after winning the licence was when we would start racing. One member of the FIA board was very keen for us to start in 2015, which would have given us less than a year to prepare. While it might have been possible to set up the team in time for the 2015 season, the chances are we would have fallen flat on our faces and it could have put us back years. The news about 2015 made me nervous: if the rest of the FIA got behind the idea our hand might be forced.

'Don't worry,' said Stefano, who was actually about to leave the Scuderia for Audi. '2015 wouldn't work for Ferrari either.'

THE RECRUITMENT DRIVE

'Then could you tell the FIA that, please?' I asked him. 'It's making me nervous.'

Fortunately, Stefano did as I asked and everyone agreed that the Haas F1 Team would join the grid for the 2016 season. What a relief! That still gave me just a year and a half to put everything together from scratch, starting with a core group of people who would become the backbone of the team. It was time to get out the contacts book.

The very first person I called in this regard was a man named Nigel Newton who I had worked with at Jaguar and later at Red Bull. These days Nigel is the European business manager for Haas F1, whatever that means, but what I needed him to do in 2014, which I knew he was more than capable of, was to keep me on the straight and narrow and deal with the detail and the boring stuff. There is no other way of putting it really. You know what I mean though: setting up companies, organizing permits and licences and writing contracts. I could do some of these things but I always needed somebody behind me with a vacuum cleaner and a big foking stick. It's the kind of job I would hate to do but Nigel seemed to like it. What a weirdo! Better still, he was good at it.

One of the next people I called was Alan Maybin, who had been the chief mechanic at Jaguar during my time there. He was now employed by the Marussia F1 Team who were about to go to the wall, and when I called him up and asked if he would like to come and help me set up a new team, he said yes. One of the reasons I called Alan was because he knew a lot of people who were currently employed in the sport. I did too, but most of the people I knew were administrators, and what I needed right now were technical people. So, when I asked Alan if he could recommend a good team manager, who again would be pivotal in helping me recruit these people, he suggested Dave O'Neill. 'He's at Marussia too,' said Alan, 'and he's a good guy.'

I'm not sure if I am getting all of this in exactly the right order but one of the next people I recruited was Kate Mackenzie, who until recently had been working as the travel coordinator for the Caterham F1 Team. Just like Marussia, Caterham had either already gone into liquidation or were close, and Kate, who came very highly recommended, was on the market. Fortunately she also said yes and she remains with the team to this day. I promise you, Kate Mackenzie could organize a busload of foking monkeys and get them anywhere in the world on time.

Making sure I had the right people around me from the very beginning was one of the things that made the process of setting up a Formula 1 team less daunting and stressful than you might imagine. I had always been a believer that in a team environment you are only ever as good as the people you have around you, and this was a prime example. Also, as soon as word got out that Haas were recruiting we started receiving résumés by the truckload. Some of the people we hired at the very beginning had to work out their contracts with other teams, but because we didn't have anywhere to put them at the time, that was OK.

There were also quite a few people who we decided to turn down, on account of them not understanding or appreciating what we were trying to achieve. I think people in F1 are a lot more open these days but ten years ago they were often mistrustful of anything that didn't mirror the traditional F1 model. With so many teams going bust there was no shortage of candidates, that's for sure, but we had to be sure that people were applying for the right reasons and actually believed in and understood the project.

Another couple of people I need to mention here are Stuart Morrison, who was and still is the head of communications at Haas, and Pete Crolla, who was originally brought in as the logistics manager but has been the team manager at Haas now for a number of years. Both these guys were hired right at the very beginning and were my eyes and ears – Pete in the garage and Stuart in the paddock. It was Stuart's job to prevent me from saying stupid things and bad words in front of microphones and cameras, so he should have been sacked foking years ago! They're great guys though. Two of the best.

The last people we recruited before the drivers were the mechanics, partly because they had shorter notice periods than most other people, and partly because we wouldn't actually need them until closer to the start of the 2016 season. Incidentally, I would say that once we had finished the initial recruitment drive, around 90 per cent of the people we hired had come from other teams so they were ready to go.

While I was dealing with that, Gene Haas and Joe Custer were busy sorting out the build of our new facility in Kannapolis, North Carolina. Luckily for me, this was about a twenty-five-minute drive from my home, but that was just a coincidence. From start to finish the build took less than a year which meant we were in there by the end of 2014. While that was going on, I started looking for a facility in the UK. The initial idea was to rent somewhere first, but when Marussia's headquarters in Banbury, Oxfordshire, came up for sale as part of their liquidation, Gene decided to buy it.

Once the Banbury sale was underway I went over to Italy for meetings with both Ferrari and Dallara. Work on the car began in November 2014, and after deciding to use Ferrari's wind tunnel, which had been part of mine and Stefano's satellite team idea, we rented an office there for the aerodynamics team. This team was headed up by a man called Ben Agathangelou, who we actually hired from Ferrari and who had recently finished refurbishing the same wind tunnel. We also rented an office at Dallara (a much bigger one) for the designers.

The person who would be overseeing both the design and build of the new car, as well as assembling the design team, was Rob Taylor, our newly appointed chief designer. After working with me at Jaguar, Rob had led the design for Red Bull's first F1 car, the RB1, and had then spent time at McLaren. I think I hired Rob at the end of 2014 so he was with us almost from the very start of the design process.

I have been asked many times over the years why the team has a facility in the States and two in Europe (Banbury and Dallara) and there's a simple answer to that. The facility in Kannapolis, the construction of which started before we won the licence, was built partly to prove to the FIA that our intentions were serious. It was certainly a big commitment but Gene was fine with it, thank God.

At that time we didn't actually know exactly how we would use the facility but it ended up housing the administration department, the HR and finance departments, a CFD (computational fluid dynamics) department – there happened to be a lot of good CFD engineers in the area – and a machine department.

The facility in Banbury was more related to what would take

place over a race weekend and would be home to the race and race support teams. It would also be where the cars were flown back to afterwards. Departments such as electrical engineering, control systems, vehicle performance and programme management would also be based there, as would the communication and marketing departments. One of the main reasons why we felt it was essential for the team to have a facility in the UK was because that is where Formula 1 run both their sea and air freight operations from.

A couple of weeks ago a journalist who is also a friend of mine asked me if there was anybody who mentored me through the process of creating the team. He was expecting me to say Niki Lauda, but that wasn't the case at all. He had obviously been fantastic in helping me get the licence, but I couldn't then go to him with all my daily problems. He was my friend, not my carer! Even if there had been somebody I could go to, I wouldn't have done it. I had to be able to rely fully on the people I had around me. Otherwise, what would be the point in hiring them? Sure, if a problem had come along that I felt was beyond me then I might have consulted someone, but that never happened. Also, let's not forget that the likes of Rob Taylor, Nigel Newton, Alan Maybin and Dave O'Neill were a lot better connected than I was in terms of the current F1 landscape, so most of the time I would just defer to them. And I did, a lot!

Without wanting to sound arrogant, by the time I started forming what eventually became the Haas F1 Team I had already had quite a bit of experience in setting up companies and even motorsport teams. My experiences with Fibreworks were obviously the most recent, and despite it being a different industry, many of the processes were the same, as was the attitude I had to adopt in order to make it work.

A far more relevant experience was what I achieved while working for Malcolm Wilson at the M-Sport Rally Team in the late 1990s. Until then Ford had supplied M-Sport with the cars but then one day they turned round and suggested that Malcolm do it himself. In order to achieve this he would have to set up a team from scratch and, bravely, he put me in charge of doing it.

'Are you up to it, Guenther?' Malcolm asked me.

'I have absolutely no idea,' I said. 'But I'll give it my best shot.'

In all we had just eight months to design and build a new car and had no facilities or staff. It was on a much smaller scale than the F1 project but there were many similarities. I also had a lot of freedom with the project. Malcolm only got involved when I needed him to. In fact, he was absolutely brilliant in that regard.

The biggest lesson I learned while setting up the team for Malcolm was that what I delivered had to be right on every level. I know that sounds rudimentary but in terms of responsibility it was a big lesson, and it gave me the mindset I needed to be able to do it again. Had I not had that experience I doubt whether I would have had the confidence to even consider setting up a Formula 1 team. Actually, I probably would have had the confidence, but I don't think I would have fared nearly as well. It's all your fault, Malcolm!

My management style has often been the subject of conversations with journalists and to be honest with you I have always tried to dodge it. It's not that I feel guilty about anything, I just don't particularly enjoy having to analyse my own personality or behaviour. It's the same as the whole *Drive to Survive* thing. The reason I have never watched an episode is because if I did I might see things I don't like about myself and start altering my behaviour. Don't fok around with perfection, that's what I think! While I always want to be a nice guy to people, I'd rather learn on the job, and I do. Or at least, I hope I do.

Although I'd had experience of managing large numbers of people, they had been situated primarily in one or two sites and I'd always had plenty of help. Now I was going to be solely in charge of 150 people spread over three sites on two continents. I did not worry about this at all. First and foremost, I had faith in the people around me who would be managing them day-to-day. What I also had faith in was my belief that if somebody is willing to work hard for me, I will always work hard for them. I've seen first-hand bosses who do not treat their staff like human beings and, to coin what is currently a very popular phrase in Great Britain, it boils my piss. People like that should not be allowed to own a business in my opinion, let alone employ and manage good people.

It will probably not surprise you to learn that during the early days of Haas when the team was being set up, if I did have a falling out with somebody in the team it was usually about money. Not my money, Gene's! Everybody was trying to do everything at the same time and the requests for money were coming thick and fast. I was always busy though, so it would sometimes take me a while to either sign things off or come back to people with a decision about something.

Our team manager, Dave O'Neill, who is from London and who looks like the little guy from that British sitcom *Only Fools and Horses*, was not known to me when I hired him and was by far the most persistent member of my initial core team when it came to asking for money. Everyone else would send me an email and wait patiently for a reply. Not Dave. He was like an annoying kid who wants you to buy them some sweets. Unfortunately, as we had not met each other before he joined the team, this was basically my introduction to him, and I don't mind admitting that he got on my foking nerves almost from the start. He was only trying to do his job, of course, but it put us on the wrong foot and at the start of our working relationship I wanted to kill him.

Let me give you an example.

As the man who was going to be in charge of the pit stops, Dave wanted to hire a physiotherapist to keep his team in shape. His initial request came through via an email and I replied to him saying that it was something I had already thought about and would speak to him about at a later date. To Dave, that was as good as me telling him to fok off, and so instead of waiting for me to speak to him he went on a mission to become my nemesis. Over the next week he must have sent me thirty emails asking for a decision. I answered the first one or two, reminding him that I would arrange a meeting about it as soon as possible, but they did not register. 'I'm going to foking kill this guy,' I remember saying to Alan Maybin one day. 'He's like a little dog that keeps nipping at your ankles.'

Alan smiled. 'He's very good at his job though, Guenther.'

'Which is the only reason I am not sacking him right now!'

A few days later I had to visit the Banbury site which is where Dave – or Dave-o, as everybody called him – was based. I arrived at Heathrow on a red-eye flight and when I landed I went straight to the site having had no more than two hours' sleep. The moment I walked through the door Dave-o was on to me about the physiotherapist. Seriously, he could not have picked a worse time. I'd been expecting him to want to talk to me and had been planning to make time. Straight away though? After two hours' sleep? Fok the physiotherapist. I wanted to hire a hitman.

With hindsight, from a managerial point of view what I should have done in this situation was look at it more from Dave-o's perspective. To me it was just something on a to-do list whereas to him it was far more important. And Alan was right. Dave-o was very good at his job, which was all that really mattered. Unfortunately I was stubborn, inexperienced in management, and was not used to Dave-o's brand of industrial-strength pester power. What made matters worse was that he was also asking me to sign off half a million pounds for some cargo crates at the time, which did not really help our conversations.

'Where the foking hell are these crates anyway?' I asked him when we finally got around to speaking.

'The company's based in Norfolk,' he said. 'I'm going to see them tomorrow.'

'OK then,' I said to him, probably glaring. 'I'll come with you.'

'Brilliant!' said Dave-o, and he meant it!

Although I was getting very angry about everything it did not seem to affect him one little bit, which sent my blood pressure even higher.

'While we're there we can go and see the company that are making the wiring rooms for the garage,' he said. 'Actually, I need to talk to you about that. It's going to cost in the region of—'

'Jeezoz Christ, Dave-o, one thing at a foking time!'

'OK, Guenther. See you tomorrow!'

He even used to give me a cheery foking wave when he was leaving the room, as if to say, 'Enjoy having your heart attack, Guenther!'

As well as wanting to see the half-a-million-pound crates with my own eyes, I figured that three hours in a car together would be enough time for Dave-o and me to reach some kind of understanding. Either that or we would just say to hell with it and end up killing each other. For the first couple of hours the conversation was quite stilted. I was still tired (I was always tired in those days) and we were both trying to keep away from subjects that we knew might start a fight, which was basically all of them.

Suddenly, when we were about forty-five minutes from our destination, I heard a beeping sound.

'What the hell's that?' I asked Dave-o.

A light then started flashing on the dashboard which indicated that the fuel tank was down to zero. Before he had time to reply we passed a sign on the A11 that told us the next petrol station was 20 miles ahead.

'Oh, foking hell,' said Dave-o.

I looked at him and started laughing. 'I can tell you one thing,' I said. 'If we run out of fuel I will be sitting in here steering and you will be at the back of the car pushing.'

'Fair enough,' said Dave-o.

After coming off the A11 at the next junction we managed to find a petrol station and so a disaster was averted – just! More importantly, it helped to break the ice between me and Dave-o and after that we were fine. He managed to limit his emails asking for money to sixty a day and I managed to be less of a stubborn idiot. The whole experience taught me one valuable lesson in management though: do not speak to little 'cockney geezers' immediately after a foking red-eye flight.

THE DRIVERS

Recruiting racing drivers was something I had not done before and to be honest I was not really looking forward to it very much. I had no problem with the drivers themselves. Most of them were OK in my experience. It was the shit you had to go through in order to hire them that worried me.

Instead of receiving a résumé like you would from an engineer or a mechanic, you might get a telephone call or an email from either a manager, a lawyer or an agent. I am not doubting for one moment that these people have the interests of whichever driver they are representing at heart, but they also have their own interests at heart, which I was aware of after having witnessed Niki Lauda and Malcolm Wilson hire drivers. Some of these people just want to make as much money for their drivers (and themselves) as possible, which should not be the only consideration, and some are simply trying to justify their existence. In doing so they can often become a pain in the ass and can either obstruct or in some cases even ruin what could have been a mutually beneficial opportunity.

As time went on I got used to this as a team principal but it never became easy. And why should it? After all, the figures you are dealing with when taking on a driver are substantial and the pressure on that person to deliver from every direction and perspective – the owners, the fans, the media, the board members, etc. – is enormous. This, together with everything else I have mentioned, can create a tense and sometimes negative starting point.

Fortunately, despite the situations I have just mentioned I always came from the position of not giving a shit about these managers and agents and treating them no differently from how I would treat an acquaintance. I am polite, straightforward, I will not kiss your ass or stroke your feathers (even if you ask me to) and I am not going to worry too much about either the political situation or what you might think of me or say about me afterwards. Seriously, guys, go and find somebody who gives a shit because if you come to me playing games and demanding that I dance to your tune, you are going to be very disappointed. Not my circus, not my monkeys.

Just for balance, I should point out that over recent years things have got a bit better and the people you have to deal with regarding drivers are usually professional and level-headed. Even so, my ideal scenario in this situation is to speak to the driver as quickly as possible. That way we might stand a chance of making progress before one of us dies of boredom.

Believe it or not, two of the very first drivers I spoke to about joining Haas were Kevin Magnussen and Nico Hülkenberg. I met with Kevin at Monza, I remember, and although I got on very well with him, Gene and I came to the conclusion that he was maybe a bit too young. What would he have been then – twenty-two, twenty-three? Collectively, the people I had assembled so far had a huge amount of experience but they had no experience of working together as a team. This made the decision to pick drivers who had a lot of experience over drivers who had less almost a prerequisite, 'How might they react to working with a team of people who are not yet a team?' being the most obvious question we had to ask ourselves. Kevin had just one season behind him when we spoke in 2014, and he had to sit out 2015. Sure, he had talent, lots of it, but that talent needed nurturing, and at the time it just wasn't a good fit.

By the time we spoke to Nico in 2015 he was already halfway through his fifth season in F1 and when we met we got on like a house on fire. 'He's the one,' I said to Gene. After a couple more meetings we had agreed terms and were at the contract stage. Then, shortly before he was due to sign, Nico called me to say that he had decided to stay with Force India. Although I felt a bit disappointed I had absolutely no issue with this, and it would have been the same regardless of who I was hiring or in what position. It was his decision, his future, and in that situation there are no rules about when you might have a change of heart or why. Had he been the only option I would have kicked his German ass around Hockenheim a thousand times, but he wasn't.

The next driver who came to my attention was Romain Grosjean. This would have been around the end of the 2015 season and he was out of contract with Lotus who were about to become Renault again. His agent was a guy called Martin Reiss who I actually got on OK with. When I called him and mentioned the role, he said he'd speak to Romain and was sure he'd be interested. This surprised me, to be honest. In 2015 Romain had finished in the points on no fewer than ten occasions with one podium, and in 2013 he'd had six podiums and finished seventh in the Championship. Even if Renault did not want to retain his services, which I thought would have been strange given he's French, surely one or more of the established teams would have been falling over themselves to sign him. On this occasion, for whatever reason, I'm glad to say I was wrong, and after visiting us at our facility in Banbury a few times Romain agreed to sign. In fact, the negotiations went so well that we had a contract put together in a few weeks. Comme c'est putain de magnifique!

In all seriousness, we really did strike gold in signing Romain. In terms of development, we needed a driver who knew the sport and the circuits inside out, which he did, and his enthusiasm surprised all of us. It was off the scale. Whether this was because he had become disgruntled at Lotus I'm not sure, but on joining the team he was like a kid in a sweetshop. Romain wears his heart on his sleeve so if he's happy, you know about it.

As time ticked on, our search for a second driver started to become a worry. I'd been in touch with about ten different drivers (or their representatives) and the ones who were suitable had either decided to stay where they were, like Nico, or go elsewhere. Not everybody was as adventurous as Romain, unfortunately. There was also a lot of scepticism about the fact that we were another new team. Not just from drivers and their representatives, but from a lot of other people we wanted to hire. Sure, we had a different business model to the other teams which was more sustainable, but that didn't mean much to some people. Those who accepted the invitation to come and visit us in Banbury were invariably won over and left with a different impression.

In the end, the man who had taken over from Stefano Domenicali as team principal at Scuderia Ferrari, Maurizio Arrivabene, came to our rescue. He suggested one of Ferrari's test and development drivers, Esteban Gutiérrez. As well as having finished third in the 2012 GP2 Series, Esteban had spent 2013 and 2014 driving full-time for Sauber. 'He's a good kid,' said Maurizio. 'And if he does well for you, we might give him a go.'

Ferrari would also provide Haas with test and development drivers for at least the first few seasons. Unlike us signing Esteban, however, that had been agreed a long time ago and made perfect sense for everyone concerned. Their test and development drivers for 2016, incidentally, were Antonio Fuoco, Jean-Eric Vergne and Charles Leclerc. And before you ask, yes, Charles did drive for Haas. If memory serves, it was session one of free practice (FP1) at both the British and German Grands Prix. In fact, I'm pretty sure that Charles drove a Haas during a race weekend before he drove a Ferrari. I like Charles. He's a really nice guy and a big talent.

I'm moving forward a bit here, but a rumour started circulating during the 2016 season that if Charles won the GP3 Series that year he would automatically drive for Haas in 2017. Regretfully that was just bullshit, and although Charles did go on to win the GP3 Series, in 2017 he entered the Formula 2 Championship and won that too. Imagine what might have been had he driven for us. His loss, obviously. What an idiot.

Recruiting the drivers was not anywhere near the final piece of the jigsaw for us, although it was one of the last things we got sorted before the end of 2015. As always, my wife Gertie, my daughter Greta and I spent Christmas at our home in Italy that year and I remember going into the holiday period feeling pretty relaxed. Touch wood, there had been no major disasters so far and everything had gone pretty much according to plan. There'd been challenges, of course, and we'd learned from them, but nobody had died and nobody had been put into a padded cell (amazingly). Best of all, the team seemed to be happy on the whole and we were still employing good people. The car was also progressing nicely and the FIA crash test for the chassis and the front wing had been booked in for early January. At least I had something to look forward to!

2016

THE TEST

Once I got used to running Haas, my Christmases became a little bit more relaxed, in that I did not have to work as much and could even switch my phone off sometimes. This was also down to the fact that these days people insist on taking time off during the Christmas holidays, which is ridiculous. Had we had an office close to our home in Italy I would have been as busy as ever.

Certain things are always sacred at Christmas, such as Gertie, Greta and I going for walks in the mountains together and seeing friends. I fully admit though that I always found the idea of everything coming to a complete halt in F1 for a couple of weeks very frustrating. It sounds crazy now but sometimes, while we were just relaxing, I'd look longingly at my phone hoping that it would suddenly light up and tell me that I had some shit to deal with. That's what the job can do to you. It's all-consuming.

For at least the first year of Haas's existence as an active Formula 1 team things never slowed down as we were still growing and refining things. This meant that at Christmas life pretty much carried on as normal, just at a slightly slower pace, which suited me down to the ground. Running a Formula 1 team is an all-encompassing 24/7 occupation, or vocation if you like, and I have no problem in admitting that I embraced that right from the very beginning. Gertie and Greta had never known anything different with regard to how much time I spent working, and with the advent of things such as FaceTime and Teams, regardless of where I was in the world we were always able to communicate as much as we ever did. In fact, I would argue that because we had to make an effort to communicate in these circumstances we would often end up speaking more than we did when I was at home. I am not advocating spending months away from your family of course, but it can work and doesn't have to be the end of the world. Not having anything to do is the end of the world, at least for me.

By the time 1 January 2016 came round I was like Nico Hülkenberg in a mirror factory. I was so foking excited! The FIA crash test was due to take place in Italy in a few days and providing we got through it, which I was sure we would, we would be yet another step closer to achieving what had now become the dream of everybody who worked for the team, which was making it on to the grid in Melbourne. The crash test, incidentally, involved the chassis being 'squeezed', and then an impact test with the nose attached. The reason this was scheduled for early January was so that if we did have any issues we would have plenty of time to work on them and put them right before the test in Barcelona. Despite this being our first chassis, such was the advancement in design and engineering within the sport that the days of teams discovering catastrophic problems during crash tests were a thing of the past. Then again, this was Haas!

As excited as I was for the test in Barcelona to begin, I was conscious of the fact that the longer you have in the wind tunnel the faster your car is going to be. Then again, more development time meant less production time and too much of the former could affect the quality of the build and the overall product. Yet again, it was about finding a balance that worked.

The biggest change from now to this time last year was that in January 2015 every email I received and every conversation I had was about either recruitment, infrastructure, administration or logistics, whereas now it was all about the car. I knew from my experiences with M-Sport that setting up a new team happened in stages and that almost invariably each new stage was more exciting than the last. In terms of motivating the team this made things much easier – not that I had to do a great deal of that. They were all professional and experienced people and knew full well what was at the end of the tunnel. Or should I say, the wind tunnel. At the end of the day, though, we were all there to go racing and the closer that came to being a reality the more animated and enthusiastic everyone became. It was an atmosphere I have never experienced since, or not to such a degree, and the difference, I think, was the level of mystery and expectation we were all experiencing. Regardless of role, everyone at the team felt this profoundly, and I for one enjoyed every second of it.

Something else I remember from this period is realizing how fast time goes when you're doing something like this. Some of the team in Banbury were fretting about a deadline and I remember saying something like, 'It's OK, we've got plenty of time.' That lasted what felt like five minutes as a week or so later I had several sleepless nights fearing the contrary. From a timing point of view, this was new territory. A million things were going on around me, all of which I was ultimately responsible for. What I learned was how easily it can catch you off guard, and at the same time that letting it rule your life and keep you awake at night can make it even worse. Yet again, and at the risk of repeating myself – which I probably will quite a few times as I am old and forgetful – it was all about finding a balance.

Haas's first car, the VF-16, was launched to the world at Circuit de Barcelona-Catalunya at 7.50 a.m. on 22 February 2016, which was the first day of the test. The name went back to the first machine manufactured by Gene's company, Haas Automation, which was called the VF1, the 'V' standing for 'vertical', which was a design designation of the machine, and 'F1' being added to designate it as being the company's 'First One', hence VF1. The press release that followed the launch expanded on this and concentrated mainly on the links between Haas Automation and the team. It was like a foking advert. 'Just as Haas Automation's products continually evolve, becoming better and more efficient,' I was quoted as saying, 'our methodology behind the VF-16 was to make it the best evolution of a good F1 car.'

Yes, yes, whatever.

Fortunately, we were also allowed to write something about the season ahead. 'Our goal with this car is to score points,' I was quoted as saying. 'First, we need to go out there and show that we can do the job, that we can finish races, that we are respected by the fans and other teams in the paddock. Then, we want to score points. That is the ultimate goal.'

Looking back, I'm not sure if I believed that we could score points with the car (at least at the time of launch), for the simple reason that I hadn't allowed myself to think that far ahead. As I said, starting a Formula 1 team happens in stages and you have to take each stage as it comes. It's like climbing a mountain. In doing that you have to concentrate on the stage you are at and on nothing else. Also, having not even tested the car yet we had no idea what we would be working with. I certainly hoped that we would score points in our first season, but did I think we would? No, I did not. My sole ambition then, which was the same for the entire team, was to get the car through the test in one piece and hopefully with some good data and positive feedback.

The livery of the VF-16, or should I say the colours of the livery, led to what I suppose you could describe as our first near disaster. At Gene's behest, the colours in 2016 would match those of his machines at Haas Automation, so light grey, white and black. I remember I put Dave O'Neill in charge of getting the livery designed and although it was out of his remit he agreed. Fok me, it took ages. It went back and forth from the designer to Dave and to Gene. It seemed to go on for ever.

'Look, I don't care what the foking car looks like,' I remember saying to Dave-o after the tenth time, 'just get it done!'

'You need to say that to Gene, not me,' said Dave-o, which I admit was reasonable.

Fortunately, before I had a chance to call Gene and ask him very politely to pull his foking finger out and make a decision, the final design came through.

'You're in luck, Guenther,' said Dave-o. 'The final design has been signed off.'

'Halle-foking-lujah,' I said, waving my hands in the air. 'Can we get it produced now, please.'

'Don't worry,' he said. 'I'm already on it.'

Armed with the design and the corresponding Pantone numbers from the colour chart that he got from one of the guys at the factory, Dave went to a paint shop in Towcester, which is near Silverstone, to have what is called a spray-out card made. When that was handed to him he immediately realized that the grey on the car looked more like silver.

'Has this been approved by Gene?' he asked the guy.

'Yeah, yeah, he's approved it,' came the response.

'OK, fine,' said Dave-o, and he sent the spray card off to Dallara who were in charge of the build.

About a week later Dave-o went over to Dallara to see the finished product for the first time and took some photos that he then sent to me so that I could send them on to Gene. When I received the photographs I had a million and one other things to think about so didn't really look at them and just forwarded them to Gene. About an hour after doing this I got a call from Gene who, for a change, was not his usual impassive self.

'What's going on, Guenther?' he asked. 'My car is silver when it should be grey.'

I have since learned to appreciate both the importance and the intricacies that are involved in preparing the right livery for a racing car, but at the time I was ignorant of both. 'Really, Gene?' I said, trying to hold back from saying what I wanted to say, which would have been something like 'I have bigger fish to fry at the moment!' 'That obviously shouldn't have happened. Let me get back to you.' There then followed a tirade of expletives that even *Drive to Survive* would have had to edit out. These were aimed not at any one person in particular, but at foking liveries.

'What the foking hell's going on, Dave-o?' I said after calling my team manager once I had calmed down. 'Gene is spitting foking feathers about his car being silver and not grey.'

'Yes, I thought it looked a bit flash,' he said, far too calmly. 'Let me speak to the factory.'

According to Dave-o, he called the guy up straight away and after asking him about the discrepancy he replied, 'Oh, yes. The grey looked a bit dull in my opinion so I went up a couple of colours. It looks much better, don't you think?'

'No, I don't,' said Dave-o, 'and neither does Gene!'

'Too late now,' said the guy. 'The car's on its way to Barcelona.'

'Oh, fok!'

After breaking the news to me – which, as you can imagine, I took very calmly, just nodding and saying, 'It's fine, Dave-o, don't worry, I'll tell Gene and take all the shit' – Dave-o started thinking of ways to put it right before the physical launch (as opposed to the online launch), which was of course due to take place at 7.50 a.m. on the morning of the first day of the test.

I'm not sure if you are aware of this, but before a test starts each team is given the opportunity to run their cars for just a few minutes in order to discover any last-minute glitches (a test within a test, you might say), and when the dates of the test are released the teams have to make contact with the track in order to book a time for this. Luckily, and because he's such a brilliant guy, Dave O'Neill had been the first team manager to make contact with the Circuit de Barcelona-Catalunya, which meant that he was able to reserve the first slot, the advantage being that if anything did go wrong with the car we'd have longer to put it right and were in less danger of losing testing time.

The team's luck continued when, after just one lap, we discovered a problem with the drive shaft, but because we were first out we had two full days to put it right. Our luck then ran out when we realized that we wouldn't be able to put the livery issue right in time for the new season. You win some, you lose some.

The day before the first day of the test I came close to having my first falling out with Gene. Up to now our relationship had been cordial and businesslike, and although we'd had disagreements occasionally, these had been sorted out quickly and amicably. This wasn't actually a disagreement though. It was a reaction to something Gene said.

I was getting ready to go to the airport for the flight to Barcelona when my phone rang. It was Gene, and I'd been expecting his call. He didn't say good luck or anything, he just said, 'Don't embarrass me, Guenther.' I thought to myself, fok me, how's that for motivation. I had worked my ass off getting the team to this stage and I wasn't happy. 'I will not foking do that, Gene,' I said. 'Is that everything? I need to get to the airport.' Had I given in to my temper I would still have been shouting at him now, but I managed to hold back. I was seriously pissed though.

Our arrival in Barcelona surprised quite a lot of people, and for a variety of reasons. Some didn't think we would make it there at all while others assumed that if we did manage to make it we would have shit second-hand equipment. This was all based on the assumption that Haas would be another Marussia, so when we arrived in Barcelona and started unpacking and setting up, heads began turning almost immediately. The decision to go down the road of investing in new or nearly new equipment was made partly because of the experiences of the former Marussia staff, such as Dave O'Neill and Alan Maybin. At Marussia everything had had to be done on the cheap, which in some cases had ended up costing them even more money.

One of the first examples I remember was the hydraulic equipment for the garage that we ended up buying some time after purchasing the facility in Banbury. The options were that we could either build our own, which would cost about £15,000, or we could buy new for about £70,000.

'Obviously we're going to build then,' I said to Dave-o.

'I promise you it's a false economy,' he advised. 'At Marussia we built one for just £10,000 but ended up having to spend a further £80,000 fixing the damn thing.'

After discussing this with Gene we decided to take Dave's advice and go down the new route, so when we turned up in Barcelona we looked far more like a Red Bull or a Mercedes than we did a Marussia. (I decided not to use Ferrari as an example there. Did you notice that? As I keep on saying, I'm a genius.)

The question on everybody's lips then, once we had set up in Barcelona, was whether we would be, how do you say, 'all the gear but with no foking idea'. They'd have to wait and see.

On the first day of the test we went out at bang on 10 a.m., which is when the test started, and the car ran flawlessly for twelve laps. Then we encountered a problem, and one that sends shivers down my spine to this day. Esteban Gutiérrez and I were standing at the side of the track watching Romain, and when he passed us on what would have been his thirteenth lap his front end began to lift. It got to about half a metre high. Esteban and I looked at each other in horror. 'Fok me, he's taking off,' I said. Fortunately, this happened shortly before the braking zone so it quickly began to come down again. Had it happened elsewhere, it could have been a disaster.

I can't remember how long it took to sort the front wing out but by 6 p.m. Romain had managed thirty-one laps in total. That might not sound like much but compared to some of the tests we had later on it was actually OK. Also, the problem with the front wing was a test in itself, and one which we had to overcome as quickly as possible. Most importantly, despite the near take-off, Romain was happy with how the car had run and said that generally the balance had been perfect.

Day two of the test was frustrating to say the least. We'd had to change the turbo charger overnight and during the installation lap the following day we noticed a problem. Unfortunately this took the rest of the day to put right, which was not ideal. Romain was scheduled to drive on days three and four but with Esteban being denied a run and us needing to do more set-up work with him, we decided to split driving duties on day four between the two of them. Fortunately, the final two days of the test went much better than the first two and apart from a software glitch and a brake-by-wire issue on day three, everything went according to plan. Lots of laps, lots of data and two happy(ish) drivers.

Notwithstanding the progress we made with the car, I remember coming away from the Barcelona test feeling extremely proud of my team. The accepted work ethic was quite different in those days, in that people were expected to work silly hours without question. While I'm glad that has now changed, the guys on the team all did this voluntarily in the early days and were as dedicated and passionate as I was. I had an excuse as it had all been my idea, but they didn't. They just bought into the dream and, after time, they started to believe in it. It was the same for me too, by the way. At the start of 2016 everything became real, which is when the hope that I had been living off for so long started transforming into belief with glimmers of expectation. Nobody ever complained and everything got done. God willing, if we did end up having any success in our first season it would be as much for them as it would be for me, Gene or the drivers.

Forza Team Haas!

THE FIRST TWO RACES

If you ever needed an accurate example of a sign of things to come for a brand-new Formula 1 team, Haas's adventures at the Australian Grand Prix in 2016 take the foking biscuit, although we did not know this at the time, of course. We went into that weekend as rookies with high hopes and fresh faces and came away feeling like seasoned campaigners. Seasoned campaigners who had been kicked in the bollocks (metaphorically speaking, I am happy to say) and then congratulated afterwards. In terms of an experience, though, it was off the foking scale and seemed to set our stall out perfectly. Hey guys, have no fear, Haas are here! We're a little bit kooky and a little bit green behind the ears, but we have a lot of endeavour, some great people, and we have no foking idea what's going on, or what will happen next. Enjoy the ride!

Although we always tried to take things one step at a time and prevent ourselves from looking too far into the future, taking confidence from what had passed was never an issue, and when we arrived in Melbourne for the first Grand Prix of the 2016 season, not to mention the first Grand Prix of our existence as a team, we were ready for pretty much anything. As the new kids on the block we also knew that all eyes would be on us, at least for a day or two. Sure enough, after setting up on the Wednesday of race week we began to receive a steady number of visitors. Some of them were known to us, such as friends or people we had worked with, and some weren't. Some people also tried to hide the fact that they were interested and would walk past the garage a few times slowly, pretending not to look.

The first VIP we received in the garage was Niki Lauda, who turned up on the Thursday. 'I need to inspect what you have been doing for the last year,' he said very grandly. 'Guenther, get yourself over here now and show me around. I want to see everything.'

'Yes, Mr Lauda.'

It was all done with a big smile. I hadn't seen Niki for some time and he genuinely did want to see what we had all achieved.

'This all looks pretty impressive, Guenther,' he said at the end of his inspection. 'I think you'll be OK. Good luck for the weekend.'

Free practice on the Thursday got off to the worst possible start when MRT's Rio Haryanto made a mistake and ended up colliding with Romain in the pit lane. Fortunately, the damage to Romain's car was fixable, although it still required a new floor. Haryanto was issued with a three-place grid penalty for the incident and later received two penalty points on his licence.

Qualifying on the Saturday didn't go much better and was a big learning curve for us. This season saw the debut of an experimental knockout format for qualifying in which instead of the five slowest cars being eliminated at the end of Q1 and Q2, the slowest driver would be eliminated every ninety seconds, the idea being that this might encourage drivers to set continuous laps rather than have one run at the start and one at the end. Both Romain and Esteban had been poised to advance to Q2 but fell foul of the new format by running out of time. As such, Romain qualified nineteenth and Esteban twentieth behind MRT's Pascal Wehrlein and the aforementioned Rio Haryanto. We'd managed our expectations well so far, but regardless of the new format this was still a disappointment. Then again, the car was good, the baseline was good, and in terms of performance we knew we had a chance.

The new qualifying format was panned by everyone but the FIA as it resulted in large periods of time when nobody was on the track. Also, drivers were getting caught out, such as Romain and Esteban, while others were finishing their runs early when still in contention. It was a foking farce, to be honest with you, and there were calls immediately afterwards to revert to the previous system. Not from me though. I decided to keep my thoughts to myself on this one as I didn't want to piss off the FIA. Not yet at least. I'd more than make up for it later!

While exciting in places, the first sixteen laps of the race went OK for us, in that there were no issues, and at one point one or two of us even stopped perspiring. Then, on lap seventeen, while attempting to pass Esteban, Fernando Alonso misjudged his move and in doing so took himself and Esteban out of the race. Until now I had managed to keep my emotions in check since arriving in Australia, but this made me lose my shit. The move had been very poorly executed by Fernando and when interviewed afterwards he showed no contrition at all. The most important thing was that both drivers came out of it OK, of course, although Fernando did have a couple of fractured ribs. Anyway, after that it was all eyes on Romain.

Although we would rather it hadn't happened, at least at the time, the accident involving Esteban and Fernando did us an almost immediate favour as on lap eighteen the safety car came out, which then became a red flag. The remaining drivers all lined up in the pit lane and as the only driver who hadn't pitted yet Romain ended up in ninth position with effectively a free stop. About twenty minutes later the race resumed, and on lap twenty-two Kimi Räikkönen retired, which moved Romain up to eighth.

On the pit wall things were changing as fast as they were on the track, as in just four or five laps I went from breathing fire and calling for Alonso's head on a plate to hailing the fact that Romain was now in eighth position with a pit stop in hand. By lap thirty-two Romain was up to sixth as Carlos Sainz and Max Verstappen had both pitted.

'How many laps to go?' I asked Ayao Komatsu, our chief engineer, who was sitting next to me on the pit wall.

'It says it right there in front of you,' he said, pointing at one of the screens. 'Thirty-nine.'

'I can't read, you foking idiot,' I said, 'I'm too excited!'

The biggest danger to Romain was Hülkenberg, who was running seventh, but because Romain had looked after his tyres so well at the beginning of the race he was able to pull away. A few laps before the end of the race Gene joined us at the pit wall. He was as excited as we were, and when Romain crossed the line to secure sixth position, and eight lovely points, we all went a little bit crazy.

As well as being one of the strongest opening weekends for a new team in the history of Formula 1, not to mention the first time that a new team had scored points on debut since Toyota in 2002, we had exceeded everyone's expectations. Mine, Gene's, the team's, the audience's. Everyone's. Gene also said some really nice things to the press after the race which meant a lot to all of us. 'A lot of people have contributed to this,' he said to a reporter, 'so we have to thank all the people, starting with Guenther Steiner, who put all this together and kept pushing me to go out and try this. The Ferrari people have been excellent. They've helped us a lot. Dallara helped us build the chassis. We've got a great sponsor in Haas Automation. It's all great. There's a new F1 team on the block and it's an American F1 team, so we're real proud of that. But these other teams are pretty dang good at what they do. I wouldn't sit here and say we're going to be in front of them all the time, but today was a good day.'

Given the fact that I considered Gene to be somebody who was very businesslike and who didn't hand out compliments very often, I appreciated these words. Romain too, who was voted Driver of the Weekend, gave almost as good an account of himself to the press as he had done on the track. 'A very good day at the office,' he said. 'This feels like a win. For all the guys who worked so hard over the last few weeks, this is unbelievable. We were unlucky yesterday but got a bit lucky today with the red flag. Still, we were able to hold off the Williams and the Force India. We didn't have much set-up time on the car. It was a case of, off you go and see what happens. This is an unbelievable feeling. The guys did an amazing job and I told them, this is like a win for all of us. First race and here we are, P6. A happy day.'

I forget whose idea this had been but before we flew out to

Melbourne somebody had suggested that we have T-shirts printed with 'Have no fear, Haas F1 Team are here'. Every member of the team got one, I think, to wear underneath their overalls or whatever, and so after the race quite a few of them made an appearance.

Something that was really satisfying for the team in general after that first race in Australia was the reaction from the press and the media. Despite there already being a growing number of naysayers within the sport, the members of the press and media seemed to find our presence on the grid refreshing, and having watched some of the coverage of the race just recently I felt pride all over again. The F1 reporter at NBC in Australia gave us what was probably the most glowing headline of all. He said, 'I cannot remember when a team has turned up so well prepared and so regimented. Well done Haas.'

The only thing that threatened to undermine our endeavours in Melbourne was the fact that a certain amount of luck had been involved. That was never the headline but it did read more like a fairy tale in some reports than an achievement. Not that I was complaining. One thing Gene had not been able to buy when we started the team was a fanbase, and capturing the imagination of the F1 faithful, which is what our result in Melbourne did, was a good place to start.

The next race on the calendar was Bahrain, which took place two weeks after Melbourne. What people often forget when looking back at that first race is that only one of our cars made it to the end (not to mention the fact that one of our drivers could have been seriously injured), and so despite the points finish, our main hope going into Bahrain was that both drivers would last the course. After all, we stood more chance of scoring points with two cars on the track than one.

Although there had been lots of rumours to the contrary, the FIA decided to stick with their ridiculous new qualifying format and the only thing that made it acceptable was that everyone was in the same boat. Fortunately, both drivers made it through to Q2 this time with Esteban lining up P13 and Romain P9.

Both started the race on super soft tyres, and thanks to Sebastian Vettel, who suffered a mechanical issue, by the end of the formation lap Romain was in eighth and Esteban twelfth. At the start Romain made up one place by passing Hülkenberg and Esteban made passes to gain three places. A lap or so later Lewis Hamilton started having problems which moved them up another position. Hamilton then recovered, the bastard, but by the end of lap one Romain was in sixth and Esteban eighth. Once again, I was sitting on the pit wall in a state of disbelief.

'Before you ask, there are fifty-six laps to go,' said Ayao, pointing at one of the screens.

'Fok off!'

Romain pitted from fourth position on lap eleven to come out in ninth and after two drivers in front of him pitted he was up to seventh. He then passed Felipe Massa and Daniil Kvyat and by lap twenty-four he was back up to fourth. On lap twenty-seven Romain pitted again, going on to his third set of super softs, and came out eighth. After passing Valtteri Bottas two laps later he passed Kvyat, who then pitted, which put Romain in the middle of a Daniel Ricciardo–Max Verstappen sandwich, Ricciardo in front and Verstappen behind.

On lap forty-one Romain pitted for the third and final time, going on to mediums this time, but unfortunately a mistake was made during the stop which cost him several seconds. Even so, Romain still came out eighth, and after Kvyat pitted a lap later he was up to seventh. Massa was the next driver to be passed by our unstoppable Frenchman, and when Verstappen then pitted a few laps later, probably out of fear, he was up to fifth.

I'm pretty sure that when Verstappen pitted there were seven laps to go and to this day it was the longest ten or eleven minutes of my life. Verstappen, who wasn't quite the driver he is today (fortunately!), made a late charge but Romain held him off and finished two seconds ahead. More importantly, he finished in fifth position, bagging ten more lovely points.

'Foking hell, Romain!' I said to him over the radio. 'Are you trying to give me a foking heart attack or something? Seriously, that was an incredible drive. Congratulations.'

Not only had Romain gone one better with regard to position, but there had also been no luck involved this time. He was also voted Driver of the Weekend for a second successive time after making eight overtakes during the race. 'Haas are fifth in the Constructors' Championship,' I said to Gertie on the phone after the race. 'And Romain is fifth in the Drivers' Championship. It's just crazy!'

The only downside to the weekend was that Esteban had to retire because of a problem with a brake disc. His front left, I think. Although further down the field, he'd been running well, and everyone felt for him. Even so, there were a lot of positives for Esteban to take from the race, not least his tyre and fuel management which had been excellent. He was also happy with the car and, far from disheartening him, Romain's success gave him hope. It was all good.

I'm conscious about using too many post-race quotes in the book, but what Romain had to say after that Bahrain Grand Prix was a great summary and encapsulated exactly how we all felt. 'This is the American dream,' he said to the communications team. 'It is unbelievable. I said we had to manage our expectations after we finished sixth in Australia, but here we finished fifth. There's still a lot of things we can do better, from pit stops to the set-up of the car and so on, but, for now, this one is for the guys. I looked at their faces last night and they were all very tired because of the amount of work we're doing. This is a massive reward. Really, just unbelievable. In the race, I had a good feeling in the car. It was an aggressive strategy, but managing tyres has always been my strength in the past. Knowing we had a softer compound for this race track was something I liked. The car was set up well for the super soft tyres and I had a fantastic race. The car has a very good baseline. Everything is working well. I don't think I've ever been as high as fifth in the driver standings. This is the first time in my career, I can't believe it.'

I couldn't have put it better myself.

The rest of the season was a lot more up and down than the first two races, with the emphasis on the word 'down'. It wasn't a disaster, exactly, but after scoring points in Russia, which was race four, at the seventeen races that followed we scored points on only two more occasions. We were almost always there or thereabouts though, in eleventh or twelfth, so at least we were usually fighting for something. If truth be known, this was probably an honest reflection of where we were as a team at the time, which was still no disgrace. Finishing eighth in the Constructors' Championship on twenty-nine points ahead of Renault, Manor and Sauber, which is what happened, was also where we deserved to be. In fact, had we been offered that at any point before the start of the season we would have accepted it without question, so we were happy.

One other highlight from 2016 was scoring the team's final point of the season at the US Grand Prix. Despite it being our home Grand Prix, and the first time an American team had taken part in the race for three decades, we had no idea if or to what degree the American public might support us. The PR machine kicked in the week before the race when we flew Romain and Esteban over to North Carolina and they got a good reception. As much as that might have helped, we were all very conscious of the fact that the one thing that was missing with regard to America and F1 was an American driver. That's what everyone needed in order to cement the relationship. In the end, the reception we received from the American public was warm and enthusiastic, and finishing in the points did us no harm whatsoever. I even saw one or two Haas flags in the crowd, which was heartening. Just like the season itself, it was a positive start.

Incidentally, the last American team to compete in the Formula 1 World Championship had been Haas Lola (aka Team Haas), which was around in the mid-1980s. The founder and owner of Haas Lola was a motorsport impresario called Carl Haas (no relation to Gene, as far as I know) who had a huge amount of success in IndyCar, winning championships with drivers such as Nigel Mansell and Michael and Mario Andretti. Despite managing to lure the great Alan Jones to drive for him at Haas Lola, they were only around for two seasons and made the starting grid on just twenty occasions. Similarities in the name notwithstanding, we decided not to remind too many people about the existence of Haas Lola as it wouldn't have inspired confidence. 'Hey guys, were you even aware that the last American F1 team before you also had Haas in its name? They were completely shit!'

THE LEARNING CURVE

Although you never stop learning in a job like the one I had at Haas, the first season was a far steeper learning curve than the ones that followed and I remember feeling compromised on several occasions. This usually had something to do with the drivers falling out with the engineers during the debrief meetings after a race.

The first time I was made aware of this was after the Spanish Grand Prix in May. The meetings took place at the top of a truck where you had the Ferrari data engineers on one side and the Haas data engineers on the other. Split by a wall, of course. We had a big table at the end of our side of the truck and after each race that's where everyone would go.

For the first few races I didn't attend these meetings (or at least not the first part) as I had a lot of other things to do. Then, a few days after the Russian Grand Prix, which was the race before Spain, I was approached by one of the data engineers who'd been attending them. According to him, Romain's behaviour during these meetings had become unacceptable.

'Then you need to foking tell him,' I said.

'But it isn't my job to start arguments with drivers,' said the engineer.

In the end Dave O'Neill came and spoke to me and he reiterated the issue. 'He's getting out of hand,' he told me. 'And nobody feels like they're in a position to say something.'

To be fair to Romain, the problems that were making him lose his temper were persistent ones that we'd been struggling with since the test, such as grip and understeer, and it was all born out of frustration. Then again, if you want to solve a problem the best way to go about it isn't by shouting at the people who are trying to help you.

First of all I had to see this for myself, so after the Spanish Grand Prix I attended the meeting in the truck from the very beginning. Sure enough Romain's behaviour was not as it should have been, but instead of saying something immediately I sat back and just observed. What had developed was an 'us and them' situation, which is the last thing you want in a team. As the sole member of his side (Esteban didn't want to know), Romain was free to vent his frustrations and opinions as he liked, without having to think about the effect it might have on other people. Or at least that's what he thought. What the situation needed, then, was a mediator. Somebody to pull the team together again. As I was the person who had employed everyone sitting around the table, it had to be me, which I was cool with.

'OK, Romain, that's enough,' I said after one of his outbursts. 'You are part of a team, and if you cannot be polite and civil to the guys who have been working their asses off to help you, maybe you shouldn't speak at all.'

The reaction to my reaction to Romain's outburst was hilarious. It was as if someone had let off a huge silent fart but nobody would admit it. It did the trick though, and by the end of the meeting we were back to being a team again and were all working together and being civil to one another.

What happened in those meetings is no slight on Romain, by the way. One thing I learned very quickly as a team principal is that being a Formula 1 driver can be a very lonely and insular existence which, because you internalize things, can sometimes have a detrimental effect on your behaviour. All I had to do was remind Romain that he wasn't on his own and that the people he was shouting at actively wanted to help him.

What else can I tell you about the 2016 season? In addition to not wanting to use lots of post-race quotes in the book, I also don't want it to be a list of race reports. How boring would that be? Without having to look through the history books or call up yet more people who worked for Haas and ask them to try and remember things on my behalf, the thing that comes to mind is the political situation that ensued regarding our relationship with Ferrari. Scoring points at three of the first four races obviously poured fuel on the fire in that regard, and after the Russian Grand Prix where Romain finished eighth the knives were well and truly out.

By far the most vocal critic of the Haas/Ferrari relationship, at least in the early days, was Ron Dennis from McLaren. First I heard a few rumours that Ron wasn't happy about it, and then one day I saw it first-hand during an F1 Commission meeting (the team principals' opportunity to discuss regulatory changes and suchlike with the F1 and FIA bigwigs). Ron got up and made a speech about why he thought the relationship was wrong. I don't remember exactly what he said but it was nothing that hadn't been said several times before. Haas are exploiting the situation, blah blah blah.

I thought that would be the end of it, but afterwards Ron decided to carry on his complaint to me personally. I'm not sure if he'd had some bad news that day or something, but boy was he pissed. At first I didn't know how to handle the situation. You probably won't believe this but I don't think anyone had ever gone for me like this before. At least not in a professional capacity.

'What we are doing is not illegal, Ron,' I said. 'And whatever you might think about it, that is just the truth. The reason we have been able to do this is because we have read the rules and regulations thoroughly. If you haven't, that's your problem, but we have not done anything wrong. The rules and regulations are there in black and white and most of them were written by Charlie Whiting. If you have a problem, go and speak to him.'

Ron was still pissed but there wasn't a lot he could do about it.

The big mistake the other teams made when we started the relationship with Ferrari was that they assumed we would fail. Even after we got the licence nobody said anything. Then, when we didn't fail and started doing well, it suddenly became an issue and everyone started wetting their foking shorts. 'Hang on a second,' I remember saying to another critic in the early days. 'We have been working on this for two foking years now, and in all that time you have been free to question what we are doing to Charlie and whoever you foking like. So why didn't you? I understand your concerns but your timing is shit. OK, go away now.'

I can completely understand why some of the old guard like Ron at McLaren got pissed about this. After all, we had spent a fraction of what they had been spending and were already competitive and scoring points. They needed to ask themselves one simple question though: if they had been in our shoes and had discovered such an opportunity, would they have done the same? Anyone in motorsport who says that they wouldn't is full of bullshit in my opinion.

Conversely, for every two critics who turned round and had a go at what we were doing with Ferrari, there would be one who (secretly) congratulated us. From memory, this was mainly people who worked for the guys at the top, so the Mercedes and Red Bulls of this world. People who were too far ahead of us to give a shit, basically.

Fortunately, the naysayers were neither involved in nor were able to influence the project directly, which meant they were nothing more than a voice that we could basically just ignore. Or at least try to. What mattered was the relationship itself.

Second only to the team of people we had assembled at Haas, nobody did more to help the advancement of the team than the Scuderia and I cannot speak highly enough about the people there. Their attitude right from the beginning helped to create and then encourage a spirit of cooperation which obviously helped both parties. I cannot remember any specific examples, but there were several instances during the first year alone when we either uncovered issues with parts that Ferrari had not discovered yet or were able to make suggestions about how they might improve. Some of these would have been relayed to Ferrari regardless, I suppose, but some would not. The difference being that because of what we had created we actually *wanted* to help each other.

Then there was the food at Maranello. Have I mentioned that already?

PIT STOP

As I have been writing this book I have realized that there are subjects, opinions and stories that I would like to include but which do not fit easily into the narrative. Any normal person would just leave these out, but I am not very normal. Instead, I have decided to include them here and there as stand-alone sections and have entitled them 'Pit Stops'. Imaginative, huh? Come on, it's just entertainment. Who cares? Either you can read them as you go as a kind of reward, or if you want to get on with the season-by-season story you can come back to them later on. Some people will probably moan that they're here at all but I don't really care.

Anyway, I'm starting off with something historical. Something that takes us way back to the second half of the last century . . .

GUENTHER ON WHEELS

There are two rumours, or should I say assumptions, about how I got into motorsport. One is that I was an engineer, which is on those stupid websites that claim to know everything but are actually full of bullshit, and the other, which I think is just an assumption, is that I had once been a racing driver.

THE LEARNING CURVE

Unlike my esteemed and very rich amigos and former colleagues Christian Horner, Toto Wolff and Zak Brown, I have never failed at being a racing driver, and for the simple reason that I have never *been* a racing driver. I have always been a Guenther. I can drive, however, and have been doing so with varying degrees of safety and success since I was fourteen years old. I was brought up in a valley in South Tyrol which is on the edge of the Dolomites in Italy, and on a Sunday morning my parents would take me and my sister to visit our grandparents. 'Guenther, would you like to drive us there?' my father, Josef, once said to me. 'I'll teach you as we go.' Well, you can imagine what I said. 'Give me the foking keys, Vater!' I couldn't believe he was asking me. I mean, would you hand the keys to your beautiful green Fiat 124 – a car that would eventually be made under licence by LADA, no less – to an awkward fourteen-year-old who has never driven a car before in his entire life? Of course you foking wouldn't. What was my father thinking?

In all fairness, I had been asking him if I could have a go at driving the car for years, and he ended up being a very patient teacher. Subsequently, I managed to pick it up in no time at all and it soon became a regular thing. I'll never forget the first time it happened. It would have been the summer of 1979, and when my father handed me the keys to his beloved car, which was his pride and joy, my mother almost had a foking heart attack. 'No, Joseph,' she said, 'he's not old enough. Guenther's just a boy!' What she really meant was: 'If you give that idiot the keys to our car, he'll kill us all!'

'Guenther will be fine,' said my father confidently. 'He's been watching me drive his whole life. Let's give him a chance.'

Before my mother could say anything else I grabbed the keys from my father's hand, jumped into the driver's seat and started the engine. What a foking feeling that was! One minute I was a slightly clumsy and overly tall teenage pedestrian who occasionally used a bike, and the next I was a young man with no less than 55 brake-horsepower at his disposal. It was a true coming of age.

The first thing I did was stall the car.

'I told you he wasn't ready,' yelped my mother, who was cowering on the back seat with my sister. 'Swap places, Joseph. Swap places!'

'Nein, Mutter!' I protested, and then tried again. As the eleven-year-old 1,438cc engine began to purr beneath the bonnet, I looked back at my terrified mother, smiled at her victoriously, put the car into gear, and then stalled it again. 'Scheisse!' I hissed.

'You see, Joseph?' said my mother, leaning forward. 'The boy hasn't even started driving yet and already he is using bad language.'

'Just a little bit more throttle next time, Guenther,' suggested my father calmly. 'You'll get the hang of it soon.'

As momentous as that event undoubtedly was, I don't remember feeling nervous at all. Just excited. It all came very naturally though and after a few trips even my mother felt comfortable in the car with me. On one occasion she even sat in the front seat next to me.

This was probably the first in what has become a very long line of things I have done in my life but shouldn't really have been allowed to, such as starting a Formula 1 team and writing two foking books. My driving style, incidentally, has merited a wide range of descriptions over the years, some of the most popular being 'perilously unsafe', 'dangerously erratic' and – my own personal favourite – 'completely foking illegal'. I've never had a crash though. Or at least not a big one. I may have caused a few over the years, but that doesn't count. Tickets, yes (more than they sell for Silverstone), but crashes, no.

The only time I have ever been paid to drive a car was when I was doing my national service. I mentioned this in my first book briefly, and on the whole I really enjoyed it. A possible life in motorsport hadn't even occurred to me then, but while acting as a chauffeur for a General in the Italian army, which is what I did during part of my national service, I began to harbour a few small dreams about becoming a racing driver. Ultimately, although I enjoyed driving, I knew instinctively that I didn't have what it takes. Actually, that isn't strictly true. I had a *good idea* that I didn't have what it takes. What I definitely *didn't* have was the desire to dedicate my life to finding out and in the process probably bankrupt myself. What I was left with though, when the dreams of becoming a racing driver slowly began to fade, was the aforementioned desire to work in motorsport. Forty years on, that desire is as strong today as it's ever been. In that respect I'm just like Christian and Toto really, just without the endeavour, expenditure, failure and embarrassment. That would come later for me!

Once again, because I am the overlord of world motorsport, there's an assumption among some deluded people that I must own a fleet of vintage Ferraris and keep them all in a warehouse in a secret location. In actual fact, the only car I own at the moment is a Toyota Tundra, which is a pick-up truck. It's big (or at least too foking big to drive in Europe), it's comfortable, it has nice heated seats which is essential for a man of my advancing years, and it's great to drive. I foking love it.

I used to own a Porsche 911 when I lived in England, which I suppose was a kind of mid-life crisis. I was working for the Germany-based Opel DTM Team at the time, so it was some commute, and for my fortieth birthday I decided to treat myself to a brand-new black 911. At first I was thrilled to foking bits with it and drove around like the Lord of Milton Keynes. Pretty soon, though, the novelty began to wear off and I came to the conclusion that it's only worth owning a car like that if you have time to enjoy it. I didn't. In fact, because of the commute I barely had time to go to the toilet while I worked for Opel, let alone take a sportscar out on a Sunday morning to drive around and look like a wanker. I'll leave that to all the retired lawyers and accountants.

2017

THE CHANGES

Something else I have been thinking a lot about while writing these early chapters is the difference between the sport when we started competing and the sport today. The fans who perhaps came on board in the *Drive to Survive* era, which is estimated to be roughly 50 per cent of the current audience, might not be aware of this so allow me to give you a view. In my opinion, F1 today is almost unrecognizable from the sport Haas began competing in over eight years ago.

For a start, Formula 1 was very cliquey back then, which had a lot to do with the notorious and not at all lamented F1 Strategy Group. Ever heard of that? If you haven't you might not believe what I'm about to tell you.

The Strategy Group consisted of FIA and F1 representatives, plus Red Bull, McLaren, Ferrari, Mercedes, Williams and the highest-finishing other team in the previous year's Constructors' Championship, which in 2017 was Force India. Nothing strange about that, you might say. Well, if I told you that they were the only people who were allowed to suggest any changes to the sport, how would you feel then? That's how it was though. Each of those teams had one vote each, with the FIA and F1 having the remaining six votes. The remaining five teams, as it was at the time, were allowed to attend the Strategy Group meetings, for all the good it did us, but were only able to vote when it came to ratifying the group's suggestions. This was carried out by the F1 Commission, which consisted of the Strategy Group members plus the remaining teams and other interested parties such as race promoters, sponsors and representatives from the different tracks. Due to the fact that all we were doing was ratifying the Strategy Group's suggestions, these meetings would often be over and done with very quickly. In fact, I remember having to attend an F1 Commission meeting in Paris one time. I flew all the way from Charlotte and I was in there for no more than fifteen minutes. God, was I pissed. It was ridiculous.

As you can imagine, the very existence of the Strategy Group used to cause a lot of bad feeling within the sport but it was indicative of the culture that existed then. It was all about control, and while Bernie Ecclestone was in charge that was never, ever going to change. Fortunately it all came to an end during only our second year on the grid when Liberty Media finally assumed full control of the sport.

In terms of what has happened on the track since then with technology and the rules and regulations, it would take a hundred years or more to explain fully what has changed. Moreover, that is nothing new to the sport. It's just F1 doing its thing. What is far easier to explain is what has happened away from the race track.

Netflix's *Drive to Survive* is often credited with delivering the change that has made F1 what it is today in terms of audience, but that isn't true. The first step was making Formula 1 more compatible with social media and smart phones. That was the start, and the reason I am aware of this is because it dragged me along with it too. Until then I had used my smart phone for calling, texting and sending emails mainly, and although I never took to the social media thing at the time I monitored the change in engagement, which was seismic. According to Haas's communications director, Stuart Morrison, who was one of the first people I hired at the team and who remains there to this day, being able to use content on social media was the gamechanger. Until then, to protect the TV rights we hadn't been able to post anything very interesting apart from photos, but during testing in 2017 this changed. Suddenly, and for the first time ever, fans of F1 were able to watch cars moving on their smart phones, and from then on everything just exploded.

The difference for me personally was having so much data and real-time information available to me at the touch of a button, which Liberty Media were also responsible for driving forward. This piqued my interest, not only as a participant but as a fan. If anything, *Drive to Survive* came about *because* F1 had opened its doors to a new and younger audience, and everyone took full advantage, including us.

Purely from a team principal's point of view, a more equal distribution of the prize fund was another positive initiated by Liberty Media. Despite the budget cap being regulated by the FIA, without the corroboration of the F1 Group the all-important changes would not have taken place. The person who has to take much of the credit for this is Chase Carey, who was installed as F1 Group CEO by Liberty Media at the start of 2017. After overseeing the acquisition he implemented the aforementioned changes and more, before stepping down and making way for Stefano Domenicali in 2020, who has also gone on to do an amazing job.

When Liberty Media first acquired Formula 1 scepticism was very high within the sport, primarily because they were an American company. 'What do Americans know about F1?' people said. 'It's a European sport.' By then I had already been living in America for almost ten years and knew a little bit about the company and their track record so I wasn't really concerned at all. Interested, but not concerned. I figured that if these people were prepared to invest over $4 billion purchasing a major sport, they were probably going to try and grow it in other countries and make it truly global, starting with, in this case, the United States. As co-founder and team principal of the only American team in Formula 1 at the time, this was obviously important to me, and I figured that the people best placed to grow the sport in the US were Americans, or at least an America-based company.

After six to eight months, the guys over in Europe began to realize and appreciate that Liberty Media were taking the sport in the right direction and so the scepticism, most of which had been completely understandable, slowly turned into enthusiasm. Even at that point Liberty Media were already doing things that Bernie either would never have thought of or wouldn't have been prepared to go ahead with. That's not a criticism, by the way. He was in his late eighties when Liberty Media took over and regardless of how white his new teeth were or how much incredible hair he had, the sport was crying out for new eyes, new ideas and new perspectives. Failing to embrace social media, for instance, at least in a way that other sports had been doing, had held F1 back and had narrowed its audience.

My theory is that during the five or ten years leading up to the acquisition, which is when things like embracing social media should have been taking place, Bernie must have been happy with where the sport was at. It was making him and his financial partners money, so why start changing, why start taking any risks? Let's not forget, by the way, that once upon a time Bernie Ecclestone had been well ahead of the rest of the world by making sure that every Grand Prix on the Formula 1 calendar was televised globally. Had he not done that the sport might well have disappeared altogether, so for that he deserves some serious foking kudos. Now, though, the tables had turned. The world was changing faster than ever before and the more it changed the more out of touch the sport of Formula 1 became. Once again, that is no slight on Bernie, as unless you have somebody you trust or somebody who is holding the purse strings telling you to change things around when you're making hundreds of millions of dollars a year, why would you? I cannot prove it, of course, but I would say the majority of people would have done the same as Bernie in that situation. If it ain't broke, as the saying goes, do not foking well mend it. I dread to think, though, what might have happened had Liberty Media not come in and turned Bernie into a multi-billionaire.

Anyway, that was my state of the nation address. What about the state of Haas in 2017?

Just like the sport as a whole, 2017 was all change for the team, in terms of the car (which I will come on to in a moment) and the people who would be driving it. As you might expect, retaining Romain Grosjean was never going to be a question for us. Sure, we'd had a few teething troubles with him, but generally his performances had been good. I've always maintained that on his day Romain was one of the best F1 drivers in the world and my opinion has not changed. The only thing missing with him was consistency. With Esteban Gutiérrez, it was different. Consistency was never his problem. The problem was that he was consistently finishing just outside the points.

In 2016, Esteban finished in eleventh position on no fewer than five occasions, and if you include his two seasons with Sauber he had pretty much cornered the market in being nearly there but not quite. Whereas Romain lacked consistency, Esteban lacked 'grunt', if you get my drift. Despite our growing disappointment and frustration, throughout 2016 we never gave anyone a clue that we were thinking of letting him go (it would probably be different these days, I think) as he was such a good team player, but by the end of the season we had made up our minds.

Finding a replacement for Esteban proved to be quite easy compared to how difficult it had been finding him. I'd just been informed that Renault had decided to let Kevin Magnussen go so I set up a meeting with him immediately. The reason we hadn't taken Kevin on the previous year was his lack of experience. Now, with a full season with Renault under his belt and having managed to score points twice in a shit car, it was time to talk again.

After signing Kevin up we were questioned by some journalists about the fact that we had two drivers who had had, and I quote, 'a troubled start to their F1 careers: shunts, being sidelined, changing teams, etc.' 'Are you hoping that their "troubles" are now behind them?' I was asked by one of the journalists.

I replied that in my opinion difficulties make you a better person and that we took them on as individuals. 'I think they fit pretty well into our team,' I was quoted as saying. 'So maybe we are a bit troubled as well.' There is an old American saying, 'What makes you suffer makes you tougher', which is what I hoped had happened with Kevin and Romain.

As well as being from different countries, Kevin and Romain were also very different characters. In fact, they couldn't really have been more different. Whereas Romain was always very extroverted and wore his heart on his sleeve, Kevin was an introvert who would let things simmer instead of boiling over. At least, initially. That would happen eventually! What I liked about Kevin when I first got to know him was his hunger to race and his hunger to remain in Formula 1. In fact, that is still what I admire most about him today because it has never changed. He once said to me that he isn't scared of dying and drives without any fear whatsoever, which I believe.

When it comes to weaknesses, Kevin is similar to Romain in that his problem is consistency. The difference between the two, however, is that Kevin's is easier to explain. With Romain I still have absolutely no idea why he was inconsistent and why he used to do the things he did. With Kevin, it was almost always down to the car he was driving. If he had a good car he'd be the biggest fighter around, but if the car was not to his liking you could almost write him off. That, I think, is linked to his desire to succeed. If he thinks he cannot succeed, it almost destroys him.

Since arriving in F1, Kevin's confidence had taken a hammering, although not because of anything to do with the above. After a promising start to his first season with McLaren he was dropped at the end of the year and demoted to their reserve driver. After then spending a season on the side-lines he drove for Renault, who did the same as McLaren and dropped him. Personally, none of that meant anything to me. I knew that Kevin had talent and I knew that he was hungry for success.

So, on to the cars.

Ever since the hybrids were introduced in 2014 there had been an issue in the sport with both a lack of downforce and with torque slowing the cars down. By the middle of 2015 this had been rectified in theory, or so the FIA hoped, by way of a new aerodynamic package that would come into play for 2017. This meant that we ended up having to develop two new and quite different cars at the same time, which was no mean feat. It also meant that we stopped developing the 2016 car about four months into the previous season in order to concentrate fully on the new car which was the future. This is one of the reasons why the season went downhill after a while. Or should I say, levelled off.

By the way, one of the reasons we were able to develop two cars simultaneously as a new team was because of the number of parts we were able to procure from Ferrari. Had we not been able to do that it would never have happened and we would have been completely screwed.

So, what changed in 2017? Well, the width of the car and the width of the front wing and the floor all increased in size, and the rear wing was lowered from 37 inches to 31. The rear wing was also moved back a few inches, as was the diffuser. In addition to this, the size of the tyres also increased considerably in both width and diameter, resulting in the weight of the car growing by over 25kg. This would be offset by an increase in fuel capacity, and it was hoped that, when put into practice, lap times would decrease by roughly five seconds.

As with everything in life, there was going to be a cost for the extra speed and in this case it was thought to be the creation of turbulent air that would make it harder for cars to follow and overtake. Then again, everyone would be in the same boat, which made it OK. Or at least it did for me as I wouldn't be driving.

I've just remembered something. When we announced that we were going to start racing in 2016 a few people said, 'But why would you do that with the new rules coming into play in 2017? Why not just start next year?' While I could understand their argument, we wanted to use 2016 as a bedding-in period for the team, so that by the time the new rules and new cars came in we would be ready. Sure, starting to race in 2017 would have given us more time and might have made things less stressful, but it would all have been too new. I've always been of the opinion that if you sit waiting for the stars to align before going for something you will have to wait a very long time. To be uncharacteristically crude for a second, you have to shit or get off the pot.

THE SEASON

The first two days of the test in Barcelona went well. Kevin was in the cockpit for both and he did fifty-one laps on the first day and 118 laps on the second, which on day two was our full programme. More importantly, all of the issues we experienced on both days were small ones and were rectified within a matter of hours or even minutes. With Kevin on board, it also heralded a new era for us in terms of driver line-up and one that I hoped would bear fruit. He was a little bit shaky on the first day and the problems he experienced unnerved him a little bit, but he was obviously glad to be out there. 'The first feeling of the car is nice,' he said to me. 'It's good to finally get that feeling after all the anticipation.' By the end of day two Kevin was smiling and full of confidence, which is exactly what I'd been hoping to see. He'd done more laps than any other driver and was working very well with the team.

Days three and four with Romain were almost identical in terms of laps completed – fifty-six on day one and 118 on day two – and on day one Romain experienced a few set-up problems, but that was it. The test culminated in a simulated wet weather session which would enable Pirelli to assess the new tyres. 'The car is pretty cool to drive,' Romain said after the last day. 'Going fast into the corners, braking late and carrying speed through the corners. I also like the tyres as they enable you to push three laps in a row.'

The second test, which took place from 7 to 10 March, went well apart from the final day when we experienced some problems with the set-up. As a result we were unable to finish the race simulation and came away feeling slightly deflated. To be honest, I think we were all exhausted by that time, which wasn't good as the season hadn't even started. Looking back, despite us being on the cusp of our second season in F1 we were still in that bedding-in period. The team was trying to prove itself to the sport and the team members were trying to prove themselves to each other. Everyone was working their asses off, in other words, and had not been able to stop for the best part of two years.

I forget why exactly, but in 2017 Haas had a short film made about the logistics and equipment that were involved in a Grand Prix weekend, and I thought it might be interesting to give you the headlines from that. After all, things won't have changed too much since then. I think what started the initial conversation about the film was the fact that the race after Suzuka was Austin, which is almost 7,000 miles away and God knows how many time zones. Regardless of the fact that it seemed like madness having two races taking place back-to-back nearly a third of the world's circumference away from each other, that was how things were and so, like all the other teams, we just had to get on with it.

First of all, let's look at the logistics, and in particular the sea freight. For the US Grand Prix, this had to set sail over fifty days prior to the event taking place and comprised 15 tonnes of equipment packed into two 40-foot containers. It was mainly the bulky stuff such as garage equipment, furniture for the motorhome and kitchen equipment. As well as being greener than air freight, sea freight is also a lot cheaper. Then again, because of the time it takes to get there you have to have multiple sets of everything, and during a season they'll be leapfrogging each other all over the world.

Air freight obviously takes a fraction of the time that sea freight does (fifteen hours as opposed to fifty days, in this case) and in 2017 we used it to send 34 tonnes of equipment loaded on to eleven pallets. I don't have the full inventory to hand but according to the film we packed in, among many other things, 144 wheels, two complete cars, forty pit stop helmets and suits, enough spare parts to build four more cars, four thousand bottles of water, two hundred radios and ninety-five members of staff. I'm pretty sure they didn't go in the crates though.

I arrived in Melbourne on 22 March, which was two days before free practice and four days before the race. I was still completely unknown in those days so could wander through airports without having to sign anything or smile into a smart phone. I am not complaining about this, by the way, I'm just reminiscing. You know me: the only time I ever said no to a selfie or an autograph during my time with Haas was when I either physically couldn't get to the people or when I had Gene with me. 'Hey, the man who pays my wages, would you mind standing over there while I do some selfies? I'll be about twenty minutes.' Our parting of the ways would have taken place a lot sooner if that had happened. You'd have to be some kind of rabid attention-seeker not to miss anonymity just a little bit though, and I do from time to time.

It might sound stupid, but after *Drive to Survive* I seemed to have a kind of silent understanding with F1 fans. For instance, on either entering or leaving the paddock I would usually get mobbed a little bit. This was fine for a while, but at the end of the day I was either on my way to work or on my way to bed and I had to go. Eventually I would start to move very slowly while people were still taking selfies, and when this happened they would get the message and move away respectfully. People almost always say thank you when I do a selfie, which is nice.

I've been trying to remember what our expectations were going into 2017. What I know for sure is that mine were slightly different from Gene's. If you're the person who has to sign all the cheques you reconcile this by expecting to see a return on your investment, which in this case means points, or at the very least us being competitive and fighting for them. For me the ambition was the same, but my expectations were more measured than Gene's. This was because I lived and breathed it day to day and had become acutely aware of the pitfalls involved and how changeable and precarious the sport really is. Gene got that too to a degree, I think, but the constant investment gave his ambition an urgency mine didn't have. Put simply, he wanted an improvement on 2016 whereas I wanted to consolidate.

The campaign got off to a worrying start when during FP2 we were ordered to remove the T-wing we had fitted as part of the new rules. It was something to do with it flexing too much, I think. We managed to fix the problem in time for FP3, although in qualifying Kevin couldn't stay on the track and could only manage P17. Romain, on the other hand, made it into Q3 and ended up on the third row in P6. This was our best qualifying performance to date, the previous one having been in Brazil the year before where Romain qualified seventh. Given the fact that he lined up in front of a Red Bull, both Toro Rossos and both Force Indias, my favourite Frenchman put down one hell of a lap.

Kevin's problems were not of his own making (he had balance issues and had not had a chance to try the ultra-soft tyre used in qualifying) and although he was frustrated about being at the back he knew the car was fast, which helped him to maintain some confidence.

I won't dwell on the race itself as it was a bit of a shitstorm for us and ended with a double DNF. Romain retired with a water leak on lap fourteen and Kevin with a suspension issue on lap forty-seven. It was not the race we wanted or expected, to be honest. Anyway, onwards and upwards.

Fortunately things got better pretty quickly, and by the time we left the Spanish GP in Barcelona we had three points finishes under our belt. Then again, we also had four retirements so we were not getting carried away. In between Barcelona and Monaco, races five and six, I had a long conversation with Gene, and this time our ambitions and expectations were aligned. 'It's about time we had a double points finish,' I said to him. 'And do you know what, I don't think we're too far away.' That was probably a stupid thing to say to my super-ambitious boss, especially when referring to such an unpredictable race as Monaco. Then again, in 2016 we had finished eleventh and thirteenth in the Principality, so why the hell not?

The 2017 Monaco Grand Prix was the seventy-fifth running of the race and as a consequence there were a lot of celebrations going on. Not that I attended many of them. I was always careful not to get caught up in all of that and preferred to watch it from afar. Luckily, from 2017 onwards, when Haas were racing in Monaco I stayed with a friend of mine called Andrea Gianetti who lives a safe distance away from the action. The story of how this arrangement came about is a good one.

In 2016 the team had been booked into a kind of apartment hotel that was a long walk from the paddock. It also felt a bit weird to me, this place – it had a really strange atmosphere. I went out one night for dinner with Andrea and he asked me where we were staying.

'You're staying where?' he said after I told him. He looked pretty alarmed. 'Why on earth are you staying there?' He must have assumed that we would be at the Beach Plaza or somewhere.

'Monaco isn't exactly shitting hotels,' I said to him. 'You have to take what you can get.'

'OK, but you know that place is usually frequented by prostitutes? It's famous for it.'

'Well, no, I did not. High-class ones, I hope?'

'I've no idea. They stay for a few months, earn a load of money and then move on. It's got a real reputation.'

'And what about now?'

'I've no idea. They might have moved them out for the Grand Prix, I suppose. Anyway, from now on, why don't you come and stay with me when you're in Monaco?'

'You mean as opposed to staying with some high-class hookers? Let me think about it.'

And so it came to be. For the next seven years I stayed with Andrea in his beautiful apartment when racing in Monaco and he was always a fantastic host. Grazie, Andrea.

I cannot remember why exactly, but we unveiled a brand-new

livery at Monaco. We also introduced a new T-wing, I remember. Qualifying went well, in general. Romain advanced to Q3, which was great, and Kevin would have too if it hadn't been for traffic. He ended up qualifying P13 but was then moved up to P11 after Jenson Button and Stoffel Vandoorne received grid penalties. Romain qualified P8 so all in all we were happy.

Kevin had one of the best starts I'd seen at Monaco and by Sainte-Dévote he was just behind Romain. Then, when Sergio Pérez pitted for a new front wing on lap sixteen, they moved up a position to P7 and P8 respectively. I think there were three or four safety cars during the race, as well as eight or nine retirements, and when we finally came up for air after the chequered flag Romain had finished P8 and Kevin P10.

With hindsight, a new team achieving a double points finish at Monaco in only its second season on the grid was an outstanding achievement, but at the time I don't think we appreciated that. Not fully. Everyone was pleased, naturally, and from mine and Gene's point of view it ticked a box for us. What I mean by not appreciating it is that the enormity of the achievement only dawned on us once we realized just how hard it was to repeat. Once we learned that, it all became clear.

In later years a double points finish became a bit of an obsession of mine, or at least an ambition. I was the principal of a team running two cars and my ultimate goal was for both cars to do well on a regular basis. Even when one of our cars finished in the points, if the other had had to retire or had crashed out that would tarnish the achievement, at least for me. Everyone in the team would feel something like that to some extent (apart from the driver in the points, perhaps) but the team principal feels it more.

As a team, we were definitely coming into our own by this time. During the first season everything we did seemed to have had a sense of urgency to it, whereas now we were able to take it more in our stride. Efficiency was the key, I think. It was a good feeling, and it allowed us to concentrate fully on being competitive and, just as importantly, reliable. You cannot have one without the other.

By the time we reached Malaysia at the end of September we had ten points finishes under our belt, not to mention four finishes just outside the points in either eleventh or twelfth. We also had just seven retirements to our name. Only Williams, Mercedes, Force India and Ferrari had fewer, with Force India and Mercedes having just one apiece.

My ambition by this point in the season, in addition to having another double-pointer or two, was to finish in front of Toro Rosso who were probably our main rivals at the time. We would need to have a strong finish though as they had secured more top-ten finishes than we had and were a good few points ahead of us. It wasn't impossible though.

An incident during FP2 at Sepang turned out to be one of the strangest things I had ever witnessed in Formula 1, and it started a year-long campaign that we waged on behalf of both Haas and the sport itself. Romain was out on the track and everything was going well until suddenly, at turn fourteen, he spun off and went straight into the tyre wall. I can admit this now, but my immediate response when I saw it was, 'Oh shit, what the fok has he done this time?' Most importantly Romain was OK, but before we could ask what had happened he said over the radio that he had lost one of his back wheels. The immediate assumption was that he must have had a puncture or something, and as they brought him and the car back to the garage we began to investigate. It turned out that either Valtteri Bottas or Kimi Räikkönen had inadvertently dislodged a drain cover at the apex of turn thirteen and when Romain went over it a few seconds later it sliced into his rear wheel. This caused the tyre to explode, of course, which caused him to spin.

Historically, when things like this had happened at a Grand Prix the teams had always picked up the tab. It wasn't written anywhere in a regulation or anything, it was just expected and had become part of the culture. As a team principal, when a car goes off you need to know exactly what or who is to blame, and the fact that it had nothing to do with either us or another driver made me angry.

'Are the tracks insured?' I remember asking Charlie Whiting.

'Of course they are,' he replied.

'Insured for things like this though?'

'Yes,' he repeated.

'In that case, I'm going to put in a claim.'

'Good for you,' said Charlie.

I'm not sure whether he meant it or not. After all, I was about to do something that could upset the status quo. Then again, the Bernie era was at an end now and in my opinion this was one of the many things that needed to change.

It ended up taking us the best part of a year but eventually the insurance paid out. To be fair, the insurance company were very easy to deal with and the reason it took so long was simply the process that was in place at the time. Not only did we have to prove which parts had had to be replaced on the car (there was damage to the floor, the wings and the suspension, and the chassis was damaged too) but we also had to prove how much they were worth at the time, which varied as to how old and worn they were. It was a complicated process, but the figures involved made it well worth the effort. From memory, I think it was about half a million dollars.

The action we took brought about a new precedent in F1 whereby it became normal for teams to make an insurance claim in such circumstances. The next team to do so was Williams in 2019. Once again it was a drain cover that had been dislodged that caused the damage, this time in Baku, and the unlucky driver was George Russell. According to the press the figure once again was around the half-a-million-dollar mark, so not insignificant. In the end, the city of Baku not only settled the issue quickly by reimbursing Williams in full, but they also made a public apology. At the end of the day the race tracks are inspected and should be safe. That's the most important issue.

I'm not sure whether Romain's encounter with the drain cover was a bad omen for us but the race in Malaysia ended up being one to forget. For the first time this season both drivers went out in Q1 and they ended up finishing out of the points in P12 and P13. The only blessing was that both Toro Rossos finished further down the order so we were still in with a chance of finishing seventh in the Constructors' Championship.

The next race on the calendar was Japan, a week later. As well as being my spiritual home (well, Tokyo to be exact), it's the race that I most look forward to each year, and it's the same for many of the drivers. In fact YouTube is full of interviews with drivers talking about why they love Suzuka. As well as being very challenging technically, you have to have cojones like planets to take it on and come out on top. Second only to finishing seventh in the Constructors', managing to score double points here would be the icing on the cake as far as our season was concerned and would give both drivers a massive boost.

Free practice was a foking disaster, but fortunately not just for us. Kevin could only manage one lap at a time in FP1 due to a water leak and FP2 was red-flagged because of a much bigger leak – torrential rain. (Torrential rain at Suzuka? You must be kidding me?) Some oversteer at turn five prevented Romain from progressing to Q2 during qualifying and after grid penalties for Jolyon Palmer, Sainz and Alonso, Kevin lined up P12 on the grid and Romain P13.

For all the talk about Suzuka being the most challenging circuit on the calendar, the race itself was pretty uneventful and all I really remember is sitting on the pit wall and watching Kevin finish P8 and Romain P9. We did it though. A double points finish at Suzuka. Gene was happy and the drivers and team were ecstatic. I too was pretty pleased (understatement of the book so far), but I had also been away from home for almost a month and was looking forward to getting back. Fortunately Austin was the next race, which would give me some time to reintroduce myself to my family.

Sadly, we only managed one more points finish during the final four races of the season, which was Kevin in Mexico, and so Toro Rosso ended up beating us to seventh by just six points. Ours was no disgrace, however. Far from it. Unlike 2016 when we scored points at five races and had no double points, in 2017 we scored points at eleven of the twenty races, so over half, and had both drivers in the points on two occasions. Not bad, huh? We also beat McLaren, which must have pissed Ron Dennis off quite a bit. In fact that was the year Ron left McLaren for good so perhaps we were the reason. Or perhaps not.

The mood within the team at the end of the season was remarkable. We had experienced pretty much every emotion Formula 1 could throw at us during the year. Frustration, irritation, anxiety, elation, pride, relief. We also experienced feelings of validation, I think, which made everybody happy and brought us closer together as a team. Most importantly of all, we were all of the opinion that everything was moving in the right direction. For me at least, 2018 couldn't come soon enough.

PIT STOP

UNDER PRESSURE

As well as being the name of a very well-known song by Queen and David Bowie, 'under pressure' also describes, quite accurately, my constant state of being since about 1986, or when I first started working in motorsport. Don't be fooled though. Being under pressure does not necessarily mean lying in bed and sweating like a pig. In fact, from my own point of view it has become an immovable part of my life, as if I did not experience pressure every now and then I would feel like I was just existing. It is, believe it or not, as important to me now as any other emotion I experience. It's what gets me washed and out of my cave in the morning.

Until I started working in motorsport, I'm not sure if I had ever really experienced pressure to any great degree. As you know, I began chauffeuring my entire family through the Dolomites every weekend at the age of fourteen, and despite my mother and sister shouting 'HELP! MURDER!' from the back seat every few minutes, unlike them I came out of it pretty unscathed. My schooling also went quite well, in that I managed to do the required amount of work and pass my exams without shitting my shorts or having to call on my brain too much. 'You seem to just sail through life, Guenther,' my mother once said to me. I did not know what she was talking about at the time, but I suppose she was right. I was fairly chilled out.

Even flunking a course in engineering, which is what I did prior to working in motorsport for the first time, barely registered on the 'foks given' scale. The course was OK, I suppose, but halfway through I felt like doing something else, so I jacked it in. At no point did I feel that I had failed in any way. As far as I was concerned, my desire to work in motorsport had simply exposed the fact that engineering was not for me, and I saw that as a positive.

In my opinion, one of the best ways of handling that kind of pressure effectively is not allowing yourself to become blinded by the consequences of things not going your way. Forget them. Just do the best you can, and if it doesn't go your way and consequences occur, you can deal with them. By worrying about it beforehand you're reducing your chances of succeeding which, when you think about it, is just ridiculous. It might sound like a very simple piece of advice but it's the one thing that will usually turn healthy pressure, which is the kind that drives you on to succeed at something and can give you butterflies in your stomach, into unhealthy pressure, which just makes you feel like shit. Why? Because worrying about what will happen if you do not succeed might (a) prevent you from focusing on what you need to do to get there, and (b) prevent you from enjoying the journey – so what's the foking point? It's something that I've lived by all my adult life, and look at me! Seriously though, I know a lot of people – hundreds, in fact – who have been so wrapped up in the what ifs that they have completely missed the good things life throws at you. Just chill out, do the best you can, keep your eyes open and enjoy the ride.

A question I was often asked when I was at Haas was how I felt when I had to call Gene with bad news, the assumption being, I think, that it must have been awful. 'That must be real pressure,' a journalist once said to me. 'Having to phone up the owner of the team you run and tell him that one driver crashed out and the other finished last.'

'Not at all,' I replied. Sure, I did not really enjoy having to give Gene bad news. I don't enjoy having to give anyone bad news. But I sure as hell didn't stress about it. The important thing when talking to Gene was that I never tried to spin what had happened and always told him the truth.

For me personally, it is quite often the small things that create the most amount of pressure, such as having to send emails. You can imagine the number of emails I used to receive during a day as team principal and the majority would have to be answered quickly. Also, I often had to speak to other people in order to get the information I needed to achieve this, so it could be incredibly time-consuming. As tempting as it is, the worst thing you can do in this situation is procrastinate. I have done that a few times in the past and each time I have ended up getting out of bed in the middle of the night to get it done. Finishing the day knowing for sure that I had seen to all my emails gave me a lot of satisfaction and allowed me to relax. Some people have a drink and listen to music. I would spend hours answering emails!

Actually, I have another example for you. After I finished writing *Surviving to Drive* I received a telephone call from the publisher asking me if I would like to record the audiobook. My initial reaction was, hell no! After all, contrary to popular belief I am not an actor. 'Surely somebody who has had training could do a much better job than me,' I said. Then I thought to myself, hang on a second. This is my project and if people are going to be daft enough to buy the audiobook then I should be the one reading it. Partly because I assume that is what they would want, but also because there is nobody else on earth who sounds like I do.

After making a few enquiries I started hearing stories about people who had gone in to record the audiobook version of their autobiography and had walked out because they just couldn't do it or felt too intimidated. 'It's seriously hard work,' the publisher said to me. 'And could take up to a week.' This presented me with a problem as there was no way in the world I could afford to dedicate a week to this project. 'Two or three days is the best I can do,' I said to the publisher. 'But let's give it a go and see how we get on.'

The pressure I felt prior to arriving at the recording studio was what I mentioned earlier, as in classic fear of failure. That said, I also had confidence in my ability (to read, at least) and knew that if it didn't work out for whatever reason it would not be the end of the world.

'Who do you think we should hire if you can't do it?' asked the publisher.

'Gordon foking Ramsay,' I said to him.

The first few hours of recording were incredibly difficult. You don't just read the book out loud in one go front to back when you're recording an audiobook. You read one sentence, then you read it again, then again, then you go back to an earlier sentence that isn't right, and then you go on to the next sentence. The process is extremely fragmented and repetitive, and to be honest it gave me a foking headache.

'How am I doing?' I asked the director guy after the first session.

'Fine,' he said almost nonchalantly.

'You mean I can actually do it?'

'Of course you can do it,' he said. 'I wouldn't have sat there recording you for four hours if you couldn't. I'd have sent you home with your tail between your legs!'

Despite the headache (which continued) and with at least two and a half days still ahead of me, that was all the encouragement I needed to get the job done. Also, the fear of failure had now completely disappeared so I was hopeful that I might even be able to enjoy it. In the end, that was a bridge too far. In fact, all that did happen, apart from the headache continuing, was that I got so fed up with the sound of my own voice that after the final session I did not say a word to anybody for about two days. I just thought lots of things instead – such as, thank God that's over with – and sent lots of emails. I got through it though, which was the main thing, and I will no doubt have to do it again when I have finished writing this book. That's unless one of these AI companies can help me out. Have they created an AI Guenther yet? As ever, it's all about attitude. Although daunting, the attitude I brought to the task of recording the audiobook for *Surviving to Drive* was open and positive, and even if it hadn't come off I would have walked away knowing that I'd given it my best shot.

2018

THE CALM BEFORE THE STORM

There was a difference in atmosphere when I started visiting our facilities and teams at the start of 2018 which was down to a sense of stability. As a new team still, that was something we had never experienced before and it gave us a perfect platform on which to prepare for the coming season. Good results are obviously amazing and are what F1 is all about, but if the place where they come from is not stable they could stop at any time. Or should I say, they are far more likely to stop at any time.

One of the reasons we managed to achieve this stability, apart from the team both having bedded in and having experienced some success, was because the changes to the regulations for 2018 were minimal. In fact, the only one I can remember is a reduction in the amount of oil that teams were allowed to burn in order to boost their performance. I'm pretty sure it was reduced by half.

The biggest change overall in Formula 1 going into the new season was the introduction of the halo cockpit protection frame, which had been developed and tested in 2016 and then approved by the FIA a year later. A lot of people cite Jules Bianchi's tragic accident and subsequent death as the catalyst for the development of the halo, but as far as I know the calls to introduce closed cockpit systems in open-wheel racing started as early as 2009, after the equally tragic death of John Surtees' son Henry during a Formula 2 race.

Since 2016 discussions had been taking place within the sport about whether it should be introduced at all, and opinions changed almost daily. As one of the older and perhaps more traditionally minded members of the sport of Formula 1, I was sceptical about the halo at first and agreed with many other people, such as Toto Wolff, Lewis Hamilton and our own driver Romain Grosjean, that it was taking the whole safety thing too far. In fact, I seem to remember Toto saying publicly that he would like to take a chainsaw to it. That's pretty ironic as the Mercedes F1 Team either invented the halo or at least came up with the first iteration. Anyway, it was a pretty contentious issue, that's for sure.

Now that I am thinking about it, perhaps unsurprisingly we did experience a couple of aerodynamic and weight distribution issues when the halo was introduced, but it was nothing that the engineers and designers couldn't figure out. Fortunately, the original idea had been to introduce the halo in 2017, so when we started developing for 2018 it was already part of the plan.

These days I equate not having a halo on an F1 car with not having a seatbelt in a road car as the fact is, it saves lives. It ended up playing a crucial role in saving Romain's life at Bahrain in 2020, which I'll be talking about in detail later. Also, as ironic as it might seem with Toto having wanted to take a chainsaw to the halo, it saved Lewis's life a year after that at Monza. Suffice to say

THE CALM BEFORE THE STORM / 125

you won't find many people in motorsport these days who aren't grateful that the halo is here, and here to stay.

It's small fry compared to the above, but I learned a very important lesson from this episode which was to be less immediately critical when things like this are suggested and to look more for the positives. Look at the HANS device, which is the head and neck restraint that is now mandatory in almost all motorsports. When the HANS device was introduced into F1 back in the early 2000s there was almost as much scepticism as there was with the halo, yet look at the number of lives it has saved.

The best way of putting all this into perspective is to read up on how things used to be in the 1960s when legends like Graham Hill and Jim Clark were racing. The reason I mention Graham Hill is because last week I was reading a book by Damon Hill and Johnny Herbert in which Damon mentioned the safety record when his dad was racing. On average, two drivers a season were killed in those days. Two drivers! With twenty-four drivers on the grid, that gave each one a one-in-twelve chance of dying. That's just incredible, and not in a good way. Nostalgia can sometimes make us think differently about the past and we often look at the days before devices such as the halo through rose-tinted glasses. People think it was cooler back then, but it isn't cool to die.

Anyway, let's have no more talk of death please, at least until I get to the part of the book when I want to kill my own drivers. That's coming up next year, I think.

Talking of my own drivers, one of the other positive things going into 2018 was that for the first time ever we had a settled line-up. What's more, despite them being totally different characters they seemed to get along OK together and were both team players. Yet another positive was the fact that mine and Gene's expectations were aligned going into the new season, which probably made both our moods a little better. All in all our relationship was good, in that he just let me get on with things and I was always honest. Apart from building a successful team that was all Gene wanted from me.

We were the first team to release images of our new car, the VF-18, and almost immediately accusations started being made about our car being a 'White Ferrari'. The usual people did the moaning, and as usual their moans were ignored by everyone except a few fellow bores and a handful of journalists who couldn't think of anything more interesting to write about. As much as I did not like people within the sport talking about us in such a way, I hoped very much that we would piss them off even more by having a good test and a strong start to the season.

With regard to the test I certainly got my wish as Romain completed 314 laps in total and Kevin 381 with hardly any issues to speak of. Romain also set a new benchmark for the team when on the final day of the test he completed 181 laps, which was the highest count of the day. Just as importantly, the car displayed good speed throughout and Romain posted the fifth fastest lap time overall. There you go, naysayers. Put that in your pipe and smoke it!

Despite the encouraging performance at the test, I was a little bit nervous going to Melbourne. Not because of any doubts or fears about the car, I was just conscious of the fact that the previous year we'd had so much bad luck there. The only downside to success, or in this case the promise of success, is the pressure it creates. Then again, it is still preferable to the pressure you experience when you are doing badly. Take my word for it.

There was one other addition to the grid in 2018 that I must mention before we move on. One that caused a lot of consternation and suspicion among the teams at first but which has helped to elevate the sport to a level it has never seen before. I'm talking, of course, about the Netflix series *Drive to Survive*.

I remember when we were first approached about this and at the very beginning the opinions were split three ways. Some thought it would be a good idea, some thought it would be a shit idea, and some didn't care. McLaren in particular were dead against it at the start as they were in the process of making their own fly-on-the-wall series which was due to be released at the same time as *DTS*, in March 2019. (Just like *Drive to Survive*, I have never watched an episode of McLaren's show but I've been told that it's a load of crap.) Despite the fact that other teams were also against the idea I don't think any of them cared enough to want to veto the series completely so it went ahead, only without the cooperation of Mercedes and Ferrari. I have no idea why they opted not to take part but it didn't take them long to change their minds. Eh guys? They couldn't foking wait for series two. And fair play to McLaren for agreeing to take part in series one. I know I like taking the piss out of them sometimes but I get why they must have been upset. They made the right decision though.

I'm delving into the realms of fantasy here, but had Bernie Ecclestone sought permission from the teams to have a film crew follow us around for an entire season and also interview us it wouldn't have got past first base, for the very simple reason that everyone would have assumed that ultimately there would be just one benefactor – Bernie. As I have already explained, right from the word go I had faith in Liberty Media. They had paid Bernie billions of dollars for the sport and could only make their money back by making it more popular globally. In other words, agreeing to speak to Netflix and then putting the idea to us had been an informed decision, and I supported it.

One thing that everybody was (and still is) agreed on with regard to our opinions when they first started filming *Drive to Survive* is that nobody had any idea how popular it might become, least of all me. If there was a chance of it making F1 more popular worldwide like we'd been told it might, then great, but if it didn't and they all disappeared after the first season, no problem.

Anyway, let's get back to Melbourne.

THE STORM

After a mixed FP1 on the Friday, with Romain having some luck but Kevin not very much, things picked up later that day in FP2 when Romain finished P6 in the standings and Kevin P9. FP3 on the Saturday was then a washout, which meant all of our attention went on to qualifying.

'What are your hopes for qualifying?' a journalist asked me while I was trying to get to the toilet.

'Both drivers through to Q3,' I said quickly while breaking into a jog. 'Sorry,' I said, 'but I'm about to piss my shorts. I have to go.'

In 2017 a statement like that would have been met with, not derision exactly, but it would have been taken with a pinch of salt and probably met with a smile. A year later it was different. The journalist just nodded, said something like, 'I wouldn't be surprised after testing,' and then wished us luck.

Approximately one and a half hours later as I was sitting on the pit wall in between our team manager Pete Crolla (who had taken over from Dave O'Neill) and our chief engineer Ayao Komatsu, the same journalist came to mind. For the first time since the Japanese Grand Prix in 2016 both drivers had made it through to Q3, just like I'd said they would. I don't believe in lucky charms and all of that superstition bullshit but just for a second I thought about going to find that journalist to tell him that I thought we would block out the front row. In the end I was only two rows out as Kevin and Romain qualified P5 and P6 respectively, which was our best qualifying ever.

You should have seen the team. Everyone was exhausted yet they were jumping around like idiots at a foking rock concert. Not me. I am an old man so I just sat on the pit wall and hugged Pete and Ayao. When Kevin and Romain came back to the pits I managed to get down from my stool with some help and after giving them both a hug I went round and said thank you to every member of the team. It is for moments like this that we put ourselves through this kind of shit year on year, and they are moments that we have to share together. What a day that was. Then again, we hadn't won anything or scored any points yet so we had to remain calm. Fat chance.

'Did you see it?' I said to Gertie later on. She'd flown over for the race and had been waiting in the motorhome.

'Of course I saw it! It's amazing, Guenther. I'm so happy for you all.'

I always looked forward to speaking to Gertie after a qualifying session or a race, whether in person or over the phone. I did have a habit of forgetting about the difference in time zones sometimes, which didn't win me any friends. She always forgave me though – eventually! Gene too had been pretty pleased when I spoke to him after the session had ended.

By the time I switched off my phone it was gone midnight, and when I closed my eyes my mind was full of scenarios about what might happen tomorrow. Luckily I was exhausted, and the next thing I remember is hearing my alarm go off the following morning.

Another reason why I was in such a good mood that day as I made my way to the circuit was because I love Melbourne and I love the Australian people. They're crazy in a very good way and they always create the most amazing atmosphere. It doesn't matter how long it takes me to get there, the jetlag never lasts long when I'm in Melbourne.

The race began well for both drivers and they managed to hold their positions pretty well for the first third of the race. Then on lap twenty-two Kevin came in for a fresh set of tyres, but after he'd rejoined the race I noticed that something was going on in the garage behind us.

'What's wrong?' I said to Pete Crolla.

'I'm not sure,' he replied. 'Let me find out.'

It turned out that the mechanic looking after the rear left didn't think that the wheel was on tight enough. Sure enough, at round about turn four Kevin was told to stop the car immediately. 'It's over,' said his race engineer. 'Sorry, mate.'

As the news hit home that Kevin had had to retire I started to feel a bit sick. How I felt now was so different from how I'd felt just a few hours earlier and the entire team must have been in exactly the same boat. This is, of course, the very nature of Formula 1 – the very nature of sport, in fact – yet I had never experienced two extremes like this back-to-back. Extreme euphoria and hope followed by futility and despair. I won't lie, it was a little bit shit.

'Come on, Guenther,' said Pete, who is another guy who joined Haas at the beginning and is still with the team. 'Romain's still out there so we've still got a chance of finishing in the points.'

Pete was right. Kevin might have been out of the race but Romain wasn't. What's more, he was running well in fourth. The inevitable inquiry and all of the recriminations and commiserations would have to wait till later.

'When is Romain coming in?' I asked Pete.

'Next lap,' he said.

The next lap was lap twenty-four, so just two laps after Kevin had had to retire. When Romain left the pit lane having been given a new set of soft tyres he rejoined the race in ninth. Once again, shortly after he left the pit lane there was a commotion in the garage and by turn two Romain had been told to pull over and stop the car. And the issue? One of the wheels wasn't on tight enough. The front left this time. I'm not sure if that had ever happened in Formula 1 before – two cars retiring within a couple of laps of each other with wobbly wheels – but I doubt it.

And so, that was it. Game over.

Despite being two and a bit years into my tenure as the team principal of an active Formula 1 team I had never had to lead an inquiry like this before during a Grand Prix weekend. If things went wrong you always had to get to the bottom of it, but this was like something out of a foking Agatha Christie novel. The first thing I did was go and speak to the two mechanics. As you can imagine, both of them were devastated by what had happened and couldn't stop apologizing.

'So, what went wrong?' I asked them.

'Tiredness,' said one of the guys. 'And the fact that we haven't had time to practise pit stops enough. It's not a good enough excuse though.'

In actual fact, even on its own that was a good enough excuse in my eyes as we simply did not have the resources to be able to practise everything as much as we would have liked. But there was another reason that, together with the lack of practice, exonerated both mechanics. At the start of the new season Ferrari had changed the design of the standard wheel nut that they supplied to us and to their own team. It turned out that these new wheel nuts were very easy to cross-thread, and what's ironic is that the change in design had been made in order to make the wheels easier to remove, resulting in quicker pit stops. The wheels were easier to remove all right. At turns two and foking four!

Whatever you might have seen on *Drive to Survive* or might have read on the internet or in the papers, the two mechanics in question, one of whom has recently gone back to work for Haas, were not to blame at all for what happened in Australia that weekend. It was just one of those things. Also, the only people who were as gutted as them were Kevin and Romain, yet each of them made a point of commiserating with the guys and letting them know that they didn't blame them. What we came away with from that weekend, which after a few days became stronger than the disappointment we felt, was the knowledge that we had a seriously good package this season. Our day would come.

THE BEST YET

In order to get the team smiling again, what we needed most after Australia was a strong race in Bahrain with no mishaps, and we almost got our wish. In Q1, after making a mistake early on Romain posted an identical time to Alonso, but because Alonso posted his time first he went through to Q2 in P15. Scheisse! Kevin's afternoon went slightly better as after making it through to Q3 again and then qualifying P7, Hamilton received a grid penalty that moved him up to P6.

Romain was obviously disappointed but Kevin qualifying P6 reminded the team in real terms what we were capable of, as opposed to me just telling them. Also, a points finish for either driver would likely put us seventh in the Championship, or even sixth if Toro Rosso had a bad day.

In the end Kevin crossed the line in P5 which equalled Haas's best finish in a race and gave Kevin the fifth top-five finish of his career so far. Romain, who tried his best but whose luck never really changed, crossed the line in P15 but was later moved up to P13 thanks to a couple of penalties. All in all it was a good weekend and everyone left Bahrain smiling, despite the fact that we all faced the prospect of having to fly straight to China with some of us having already been away from home for over three weeks.

Over the next six races, so from China to France in June, Kevin's form continued. At three of the races he scored points and at the other three he finished just outside. Romain, on the other hand, never really recovered from what happened in Australia and his form took a dive, to the point where he eventually became a liability. Two examples spring to mind, one that was probably down to carelessness and one that beggars belief and was down to I still don't know what. I'll do them in chronological order, which means the last one first.

The Grand Prix in Baku was the race in question. Despite having had to start the race from the back of the grid Romain was running P6. This is it, I thought. Things are starting to turn. Towards the end of the race the safety car came out for a few laps, which was good news for us as we could almost smell the points. Then, while warming up his tyres on the run down to turn fifteen, Romain inexplicably went straight into the barriers. Yes, you read that correctly: he crashed under the safety car. I know I like to swear every now and then but once the TV cameras had all disappeared from the vicinity I went foking mental. Not in front of Romain or anyone. That would have done no good whatsoever. I just needed to let off some steam.

The most realistic scenario for what might have happened that day is that we would probably have finished P5 or P6, because at the time of crashing Romain was in a battle with Sergio Pérez – a battle he could very well have won – who ended up finishing on the podium. That was a tough one to take.

Next up was the Spanish Grand Prix at which both drivers once again got through to Q3 (despite Romain spinning into the gravel in FP2 and FP3) with Kevin then qualifying P7 and Romain

P10. Yet again, I remember sitting on the pit wall and praying that this would be the beginning of Romain's season. In fact I actually had a good feeling about this one and something told me that Romain was going to do well. Unfortunately my prayers were not answered and my feelings turned out to be foking liars as at turn three on the opening lap Romain spun off into the middle of the track causing a smokescreen which took out Pierre Gasly and Nico Hülkenberg and triggered a safety car that lasted six laps.

'Well, at least it cannot get any worse,' Gertie said to me when I called her that night.

'Don't hold your breath,' I replied. 'It's Monaco next.'

That might have sounded flippant but I actually meant it. Romain was so desperate to put things right that he had started taking even more risks than usual. When you're in that frame of mind at Monaco, anything can happen.

The first thing I remember about the Monaco Grand Prix weekend in 2018 is the Spanish incident coming back to bite Romain on the backside. After qualifying P15 in Q1, which normally would have put him through to Q2, he received a three-place penalty for the crash in Barcelona which put him in P18 and so out of the running.

The race itself was awful. We could not find any pace and despite not crashing out, which I suppose was a bonus, Romain finished P15 and Kevin P13. The only other silver lining I could think of at the time regarding Romain was that the French Grand Prix was just a month away. It's surprising, but although he had already been racing in Formula 1 for almost a decade the French Grand Prix hadn't been running during that time so this would be his debut.

'If anything can put him back on the right track,' I said to Ayao, 'surely this can.'

'Let's hope so.'

Did either of us think it would happen? Probably not. I was in a similar position to Romain, I suppose, in that I was so desperate for things to change that my judgement had been affected.

In the end, all that France did was expose the gap that had been created between Kevin and Romain, in terms of both points and how they drove. Kevin was ballsy and oozed confidence, whereas Romain had no confidence and just whinged all the time. Instead of taking stupid risks he had now started blaming other drivers. While that was obviously a cheaper alternative to crashing, it was no less frustrating.

While Romain had been imploding, Kevin had been going from strength to strength, and when we left France for Austria he was lying an impressive eighth in the Drivers' Championship which was the highest he'd ever been. Haas were now lying sixth in the Constructors' but were fighting a different team. Actually, we were fighting two. Toro Rosso's season already appeared to have flatlined and the two teams that were just above us in fourth and fifth were Renault and McLaren. McLaren were definitely beatable as after a strong start to the season they were starting to show frailties, but Renault were the real deal. By the time the F1 circus started arriving in Austria they had no fewer than five double points finishes to their name, which was very impressive. Despite this I was confident that if we could just get Romain up and running we would be in with a chance of at least matching them. Then, if their luck ran out, who knows?

Incidentally, although he had spent a lot of time moaning over the radio, Romain had finished P11 in France which was his best finish of the season. It still wasn't where he wanted to be of course, or where we wanted him to be, but it appeared to have galvanized him.

After that build-up I suppose you are expecting me to tell you that something incredible happened in Austria. Well, it did, because immediately after FP2 we were fined €5,000 for having released Kevin from his pit box with – would you foking believe it – a loose wheel! Boy, that was shit.

'Is there any way we can just change the tyres and not the wheels?' I said to Pete Crolla.

'Sure,' he said, 'if you're happy having fifteen-minute pit stops.'

Things picked up pretty quickly when just a few hours later both drivers advanced to Q3. Even with Kevin flying like he was, I could tell that this was going to be Romain's weekend. He qualified an impressive P6 (Kevin P8) but then moved up to P5 thanks to a penalty for Vettel. With so many strong cars in the rows just behind I had no idea how things might go and the whole thing was in the lap of the gods. Getting this far had been an achievement in itself but as always it would mean nothing if we couldn't convert it into points.

Fortunately the gods were smiling down on us that day as thanks partly to the retirement of both the Mercedes cars that had blocked out the front row in qualifying and a couple of well-timed safety cars, not to mention some incredible tyre management by both drivers, Romain crossed the line in P4 and Kevin P5. Incidentally, this was Haas's fiftieth Grand Prix so the timing couldn't have been better.

'How are you feeling now, Romain?' I asked when he got to the garage.

'Pretty relieved,' he said. 'I was beginning to wonder if I still had it in me.'

'In you to what, crash out? Look, Romain, everybody in the team knows how good you are and you're also a nice guy, which is why everybody wants to see the old Romain back again. We know you can do it.'

Looking back, this entire episode brought home once again how lonely life can be when you're a racing driver. When things are going your way and you get everything right I'm sure it can be amazing, but when it doesn't and you're in the shit it must be just that – shit. Anyway, it was good to see Romain finally coming out the other side.

The result in Austria moved Haas up to fifth in the Constructors', which for a team that had only been on the grid for two and a half seasons was pretty impressive. As expected, the result also gave leave for some of the whingers to start up the White Ferrari thing again, but I don't think anyone was really interested. They were whingeing into an echo chamber.

I figured that as long as we had an association with Ferrari the accusation would carry on making an appearance every time we did well, so I was obviously hoping for more of the same. Normally I don't like listening to people who moan a lot – in fact, I usually hate it – but this was turning into pure poetry.

THE BEANS

It's safe to say that, especially during the latter part of our relationship, Gene and I had one or two differences of opinion about what he should spend money on. I'll come on to the more serious stuff later in the book, but in 2018 after the Austrian Grand Prix we had a disagreement about something that wouldn't have looked out of place in a bad sitcom.

At the time Gene had recently bought a 7X business jet. It held up to sixteen people and had a range of over 6,000 miles so could make it from London to LA easily. After the Austrian Grand Prix I was due to travel back with Gene from Austria to Banbury for some meetings and then he would fly back to the States the following day. 'Jeezoz, this is an impressive piece of kit,' I said to him as we arrived at the airport. I stopped short of asking how much it had cost him but made sure I Googled it later on. Between $18 million and $32 million, it said.

The airport we used was a private one situated close to the circuit and we were due to fly into Luton, which is about 60 miles from Banbury. As we sat in the departure area at the airport I mentioned to Gene in passing that I was hungry. 'With all of that excitement I forgot to eat at the track,' I said to him. 'In fact, I haven't eaten a thing since breakfast. What are we having on the plane?'

'Oh, I haven't booked any catering,' he said nonchalantly.

'What, nothing? Not even a drink? It's a three-hour flight. I need food, Gene!'

My appeal was met with a stony silence. I didn't understand it. Why the fok would you spend millions on a plane but then not put any food or drink in it? It didn't make sense to me.

'OK, do you mind if I try and organize something quickly?' I said.

'Why?'

'Because I'm starving!'

I could tell that Gene wasn't happy but the alternative was spending three hours with a hungry Italian at 32,000 feet, which is a fate that I would not wish on my worst enemy. 'OK, go ahead,' he said reluctantly.

Luckily we still had well over an hour until take-off so I made a telephone call to the Haas catering guys who were still at the track.

'Leave it to me,' said John, the manager. 'I'll bring something over personally.'

'Thank you, John,' I said. 'You have just helped to avert an angry disaster!'

About ten minutes after we boarded the plane I saw John emerge from the departure area carrying a large deep silver catering tray. 'Look at that,' I said to Elizabeth, who was my assistant at the time and was travelling with us. 'There must be enough food in that to feed twenty people. God, I'm hungry!'

I didn't even ask what was in there, and when John disembarked the plane having deposited the tray in the galley I looked at it longingly. As soon as we were airborne it would be all mine.

Well, at least half of it would be. Gene and his friend who was also travelling with us weren't hungry.

About five minutes after take-off the seatbelt signs finally went off. 'Do you want me to get you some?' I said to Elizabeth.

'No, it's OK, I ate at the track.'

'Lucky you!'

Whatever it was it was still hot, and by the time I went to lift the lid up I was literally salivating.

'What the fok? You have to be joking!'

'What's the matter?' said Elizabeth, running to the galley and looking in the tray. 'Oh, I see. Oh dear. That's not very appetizing, is it?'

Instead of taking what was left of a nice lasagne or a casserole, John had acquired a full tray of baked beans.

'I foking hate baked beans,' I said, looking miserably at the tray. 'And even if I didn't, I'm not sure that eating a tray of them in a confined space would be a very good idea. Remember the film *Blazing Saddles*?'

Elizabeth nodded. 'Yes, there'd be no escape, would there? It must have been all they had left. You'll have to wait until we get to Banbury.'

'What, in three hours? I could eat a scabby goat at the moment.'

'Not beans though?'

'Fok off.'

When we landed in Luton the first person to get up from their seat was Gene. During the flight he'd got up to inspect the food but, like me and Elizabeth, had decided against consuming any of it.

'Guenther, could you collect the tray of beans as you leave the plane please,' he said to me. 'I'd like to take them back to the factory.'

'But why?' I asked.

'I don't want them to go to waste. The boys in the shop can have them.'

'The boys in the shop can have them? So you want me to take this tray of baked beans back to my hotel room, put them to bed and then take them to the factory with me tomorrow and present them to the boys in the shop?'

I looked at Elizabeth and she looked at me. Neither of us could believe it.

'But Gene,' I continued, 'they've been stinking the whole plane out for the last three hours. And how are we going to get them to Banbury?'

'The lid's on tight enough,' he said. 'You can carry them.'

Beangate had now officially begun.

After getting off the plane we walked through Arrivals – very slowly, of course, as I was carrying an enormous tray of foking beans – and made our way to the car. Because I don't like beans the smell in the plane had made me feel a bit nauseous, but that was nothing to how they made me feel in the confines of the car.

'Would you like me to take those?' Elizabeth asked. She could see that I was in danger of projectile vomiting.

'It's OK,' I said bravely, 'but you can open a window.'

As Elizabeth opened the window I looked over at Gene. Since leaving the track he'd been on his phone constantly, answering emails, and although it was his suggestion he seemed to be oblivious to the ridiculousness of the situation.

When we arrived at the hotel Gene went off to make a

telephone call while I, Elizabeth and Gene's friend walked towards reception. Well, they did. I started to make a detour towards the restaurant where I intended to find the kitchen and somebody who might be willing to dispose of Gene's beans.

'I hope you're not looking to dump the beans?' said Gene's annoyingly loyal friend as I veered off. 'He'll be seriously pissed if you do.' His friend then walked off, which left just me and Elizabeth.

'Elizabeth, I think you should have these,' I said, trying to hand her the beans.

If looks could kill I'd have exploded into a million pieces there and then.

'OK then,' she said, taking them.

I couldn't believe it! Freedom from Gene's foking beans!

'Thank you, Elizabeth,' I said. 'I won't forget this.'

The reason Elizabeth took the beans was because she'd thought of a way of getting rid of them, which was to leave them on a table close to reception and then conveniently forget them. And it worked like a dream. Well, almost.

'Miss? Excuse me, Miss!' came a cry from one of the receptionists as we walked towards the lifts. 'You've forgotten your food!'

Elizabeth was not happy. 'Oh, bollocks,' she hissed. 'This is all your fault.'

'It's not!' I said. 'They're Gene's beans, not my beans!'

As funny as it sounds, the situation was becoming annoying so I decided to bring Beangate to an end once and for all. 'Give them to me,' I said, taking the tray. 'I'll take them upstairs, wait twenty minutes, and then bring them downstairs and just dump them somewhere.'

'Are you sure?' said Elizabeth.

'I am, and if Gene catches me or asks about them in the morning, he can foking sack me.'

He didn't do either, by the way.

'Aren't you going to get something to eat?' Elizabeth asked as we walked towards the lifts.

'No, I think I've been put off food for ever,' I said.

THE DISQUALIFICATION

'The FIA have disqualified Romain? You're kidding me, right?'

'No, I'm afraid not.'

'And who put in the complaint?'

'Who do you think? They complained that the floor was illegal due to it flexing excessively.'

'This is all bullshit. I am going to foking speak to the FIA.'

'That'll only make things worse. A lot worse. We can appeal officially, of course, but doorstepping them and shouting the odds now isn't going to help our cause.'

'Then we foking will appeal.'

At the four Grands Prix after Austria – the British, the German, the Hungarian and the Belgian – we had got six points finishes including two doubles which was twice as many as Renault. We were still behind them in the Constructors' but only by a couple of points, and if the form of each team at the last four races continued we'd have fourth place in the bag. From memory, the difference in prize money between fourth and fifth in 2018 was only about $3 million, but there was more to it than that. It would send a huge message out to the sport of Formula 1 and would have the White Ferrari brigade spitting foking feathers and throwing all of their little pink toys out of their prams. Not that I wanted to wind these people up or cause any trouble, of course. I would never do anything like that. No, never.

The race after Spa was Monza. Kevin, who had scored points at eight of the thirteen races so far, had some bad luck and finished out of the points in P16. Romain, on the other hand, who had now moved up to fifteenth in the Drivers' Championship after having been down in nineteenth since almost the start of the season, put in a good shift and finished P6. The two Renault drivers finished P13 and P8 in the race which was enough to put us into fourth in the Constructors' Championship.

The only thing that stopped me from celebrating this after the race was a nagging feeling that the FIA might be knocking on our doors pretty soon, and unfortunately I had good reason. In between Silverstone and Hockenheim the FIA had requested that the teams make changes to the floors of the cars in time for the Italian Grand Prix as part of a new technical directive. We were having problems with our suppliers at the time and with the summer break about to take place (the FIA's sporting regulations state that all teams must observe a period of fourteen consecutive calendar days during the months of July and/or August when they cease operations, partly to keep costs down but also to allow team members to recuperate) we had asked the FIA for a period of grace and had said that we could make the changes in time for Singapore, in mid-September. While the FIA claimed to understand our situation they would not budge and said that running an unmodified floor would leave it open to a protest from a rival team. You know what's coming next, I suppose.

Sure enough, about ten minutes after the race had ended I was told that Renault had lodged a complaint about us running with an illegal floor. It was expected, but it obviously wasn't welcome, and when the complaint came in I hit the foking roof. Why? Oh, I don't know. Suddenly being fourth and then having it taken away from us might have had something to do with it. It was a hard pill to swallow at the time and I wanted blood. Renault- and FIA-flavoured blood, of course. My favourite kind at the time.

'We do not agree with the stewards' decision to penalize our race team,' I said in a statement that evening, 'and we feel strongly that our sixth-place finish in the Italian Grand Prix should stand. We are appealing the stewards' decision.'

A few days later we were informed by the FIA that the appeal would take place at their headquarters in Paris almost two months after the race in question, on 1 November. In the meantime there was the small matter of six more races, which meant that by the time the appeal was heard our fight for fourth could be all over for us. Then again, it might not. The cost of lodging an appeal was going to be about a quarter of a million dollars, which would go mainly on lawyers' fees, but at the time Gene and I felt that, given what was at stake, we had to give it a go.

On 1 November the appeal was rejected by the FIA and by that time Renault had created a forty-point gap between us in the Championship. As far as I know, in the majority of Western countries when somebody appeals a sentence that has been handed down in a criminal court, the appeal will be heard by a judge different from the one who passed the sentence. Otherwise, how can that appeal be impartial? With Formula 1 it's different, so if a sentence gets handed down by the FIA and you decide to appeal, they are the ones who will hear that appeal and make a final decision. It's the same in quite a few sports, I think, and makes true impartiality almost impossible.

Despite what I think about the appeals process at the FIA, with hindsight we should not have appealed their decision to disqualify us at Monza. What we should have done instead was moved heaven and earth to have the floor changed in time for the race, as they had requested. I'm still not sure whether we could have made it in time, but we could probably have done more to improve our chances. In our defence, we were lacking in experience in those days, but it ended up being an important lesson for us.

The most important thing after losing the appeal was to try and finish the season on a high, and we managed to do just that with two double points finishes – a P8 and P9 in Brazil and a P9 and P10 in Abu Dhabi. Renault managed just one points finish in those races and two retirements. Then again, they still finished fourth in the Constructors' and by a margin of twenty-nine points, so even if we had won the appeal it would not have made any difference. Right from day one, as well as being reliable, our car had been the fourth fastest on the grid in 2018. Unfortunately a general lack of experience, not to mention some costly errors by both the team and the drivers, had prevented us from exploiting the fact as much as we should have. There you go. Shit happens.

OK, and now for a more positive perspective. I'm pretty sure I have used this line already, but had somebody told me on getting our licence that after three years of competing we would have the fourth fastest car on the grid and would end up finishing fifth in the Constructors' Championship, I would have called

Nurse Ratched and asked her to administer some medication. I think Gene and I had talked about producing a five-year plan at the beginning of the project but it went out of the window almost immediately. We knew where we'd like to be in five years, but with all the regulation changes coming up when we started it was almost impossible to look beyond the first season, at least with any kind of clarity.

The other thing that prevents you from looking so far ahead in F1 is that you have no idea what everyone else is doing. I wish to hell you did, but you don't. From a team principal's point of view that's a pain in the ass, but from a spectator's point of view it's exactly what you want. In soccer, every team knows how strong each team is likely to be at the start of the season based on which players they have bought or already have in place. It isn't an exact science, but everything is laid bare and, apart from the odd irregularity, you have a good idea of what's going to happen. In F1 you still have an expected hierarchy based on who is already in situ, but from a technical point of view everything is very closely guarded and surprises can occur. It's one of the things people love about F1, and as the sport evolves technically, so too do the mystery and anticipation. All they need to do now is clone Adrian Newey and give each team a shiny new one. Then things would get *really* interesting.

One last thing I remember about the end of the 2018 season is the succession of post-mortems that took place regarding the camera crews from *Drive to Survive*, which was due to be released the following March. Some people complained about the amount of time that had been taken up doing interviews, and others complained that the film crews had been too intrusive. From my own point of view, and I'm pretty sure this was the same for the rest of the guys in the team, after the first couple of races we got to know the *DTS* guys pretty well and they were fun. I also don't remember them getting in the way, and if I needed them to fok off for a bit, which I did from time to time if I was talking about something confidential with Gene for instance, they did as I asked and foked off. Lastly, as somebody who has always liked new experiences and who had never been involved in anything like this before, I found it interesting and at times quite exciting.

What everyone was waiting for now, of course, was how the series would be received by the general public, which would obviously determine whether the film crew and the horrific amount of inconvenience, intrusion, chaos and hell they brought with them would return next season. Either way, I remember remarking to our communications director Stuart Morrison that as Formula 1 was still a niche sport, the audience would be limited.

'Exactly,' he said. 'It's not as if it's going to turn you all into celebrities.'

'Fok me,' I said to him. 'Can you imagine? The world does not need that at the moment.'

PIT STOP

THE EGOS HAVE LANDED

If somebody ever tells you that they do not have an ego, take my word for it, they are talking bullshit. People like to have their feathers stroked from time to time, and that includes everyone. It includes you and it includes me. It is also an essential tool for getting on in life. If it wasn't for my ego I wouldn't have had the confidence to ditch my engineering course halfway through and seek a career in motorsport, which means it has a hell of a lot to answer for! Getting to know your ego and then improving it and using it to your advantage is a skill worth learning in my opinion, but what you have to be very careful of is not allowing it to grow too big. Or, in layman's terms, do not allow yourself to become an egocentric prick. In fact, before I move on, let me give you some tips on how to keep your ego in check and make it work for you.

The first thing that happens when you become an egocentric prick is that you lose sight of reality. For instance, if I was an egocentric prick then I would either laugh off any and all criticism that was levelled at me or lose my shit and treat with contempt the people who were dishing it out. Fortunately, I was big enough to know that some of the criticism levelled at me in my role as team principal was justified and my ego allowed me to accept the fact and even learn from it. It also allowed me to admit when I made mistakes, which in turn gave me the opportunity to put things right. Sometimes it took me a while to realize that I had made a mistake but I got there in the end.

In Formula 1, the egos are probably a little bit bigger than average, which is to be expected. After all, if you had a job that was the envy of lots of people around the world and had hordes of fans kissing your ass and telling you how fantastic you are on social media all the time, it might start to affect you. The trick to not becoming a wanker is to not believe the hype and remember that at the end of the day you are just a human being. Some people are definitely more successful at this than others.

So, how do you handle people who believe the hype and think that they are God's gift? Well, why not try the Guenther Steiner method? I had to deal with quite a few egotistical people during my time at Haas and what worked for me was treating them exactly the same as I treated everybody else and making no allowances. I could not give a shit if somebody thinks they are amazing and better than other people. If I think you are amazing I will tell you, but I will also tell you if I think you are a prick.

I had this discussion with one of the Haas engineers a few years ago and he made the suggestion that not pandering to the whims of people with big egos, or at least stroking their feathers, might be bad for business.

'Tough shit,' I said to him. 'There are some things I will not budge on regardless of the circumstances, and that is one of them.'

'But if a driver you wanted to sign had a big ego,' he said, 'wouldn't you alter your behaviour just a little bit?'

'No way!'

I think he thought I was crazy, but it wasn't just me I had to think about. I had to think about the team. People with inflated egos make other people feel uncomfortable and I didn't want that shit. A driver, regardless of how famous or talented they are, is part of a team, and at Haas that was always non-negotiable. I'd sooner have no success at all than have success with a driver who is not respected by the people who have helped them achieve it. They don't all have to be best friends, but there needs to be a mutual understanding and respect in place, otherwise it's unhealthy.

Also, by indulging these people you are actually making them worse as you're adding to the legend they are creating for themselves. By not indulging them you are doing them a favour. That's the way I look at it. There have been times when I have had egotistical people forced upon me in the work environment (before Haas) and it's always been awkward. First of all for them, as they didn't like the fact that I wouldn't kiss their ass, and then for me, as I got fed up with trying to avoid them all the time.

When I first told the publishers that I wanted to write a chapter about egos they all started shitting themselves and calling in the lawyers.

'You're not going to name names, are you?' they said.

'That all depends,' I replied.

'On what?'

'On what kind of mood I'm in when I write the chapter.'

'Really?'

'No, of course not! If I named all the people I've met in Formula 1 who I think have a big ego I would have my ass sued and would be bankrupt within a foking month.'

'Thank God for that,' they said. These people are so panicky sometimes.

In my experience, the people with the biggest egos are quite often the ones who have the most to prove, and the reason they have a big ego is that they're not where they would like to be. They're insecure, basically. The people who have made it are often more comfortable and as a result their egos are in check. Once again, this is not an exact science. In fact it's just an observation, really. A factual one. Sorry, that was my ego talking.

Perhaps a more interesting observation is the fact that some people break the mould by appearing not to have an ego at all, yet when you get them on to a racing track they become an animal. I think there are a lot of these people on the grid at the moment. Look at Zhou Guanyu. I don't know the guy but he's pretty unassuming and if you met him at a party and had to guess what he did for a living you probably wouldn't say 'Formula 1 driver'. There are other drivers who are quiet, such as Kevin and Valtteri Bottas, but they have an air about them. I have to be honest though, when I started writing this chapter I had to really think about it because I look at these guys as drivers first and foremost. Take Daniel Ricciardo. He is without doubt one of the biggest characters in the sport, but when I hear his name or see him in the paddock that isn't what comes to mind. I see the driver first. The guy who has won eight Grands Prix and has made it on to the podium thirty-two times. Why? Because the paddock is a place of work and we're there to do a job.

Most people I've met who are at the very top of their profession, whether they are a racing driver or a rock star, will usually have a certain swagger about them which signifies a confidence in their ability. 'Here I am,' they're saying, 'and I'm the foking GOAT!' An extreme yet slightly alternative version of that would be the Irish mixed martial artist Conor McGregor, who I met in Monaco in 2022. Extreme because when he walked into the garage it was like meeting the world's most successful person, and slightly alternative because he has an ego the size of the solar system. The difference being that having an ego is an essential part of what he does for a living, *and* he can back it up.

Talking of backing it up . . . look at Fernando Alonso. When he retired in 2018 I remember reading lots of articles about his ego potentially having prevented him from becoming one of the most decorated Formula 1 drivers ever. 'As the years ticked on,' one journalist wrote, 'Fernando's task was to not extend his legacy, it was to repair it.' There are two sides to every story of course, and I am sure that when Fernando's autobiography eventually comes out after he retires again in 2055 we will hear his side of the story. What I know for sure though is that his comeback has been one of the greatest success stories in recent times and just about everybody has had to take a step back and re-evaluate things.

This is just my opinion, but in addition to winning the World Endurance Championship while he was out of Formula 1 and becoming a two-time Le Mans winner, Fernando learned how to make his ego work for him, which perhaps he did not do so well in the years before. And look at him now. He's quiet, self-assured and conducts himself immaculately, which means he can put all of his emotional and physical energies into being brilliant on the track. He's very much like Lewis Hamilton in that respect. I recently read an interview with the former F1 driver Christian Danner, who is a good friend of mine, in which he said that Lewis had to have his ego flown in on a jumbo jet. In my experience that has never been the case. Lewis has got all the clothes and the famous friends, but his behaviour has always been exemplary. He's a sophisticated and classy dude.

A few weeks ago I read an article by the F1 journalist Rebecca Clancy (I've been doing a lot of reading lately!) in which she said that after having been asked by Lewis what it was like being a woman in F1 and then informing him that at the media hotel in Saudi Arabia women weren't allowed to use the pool or the gym, he had a word and made sure that they could use the facilities. There's a difference between having a big ego and using your influence to do something good.

Talking of sophisticated and classy guys . . . a few years ago I inadvertently made a comment about the ego on a certain Netflix show about Formula 1 and afterwards people started putting it on foking T-shirts! I used to think it was just my comment about Kevin not 'fok smashing' my door that people were interested in, but apparently not.

'You'll never guess what's happened?' Stuart Morrison said to me one day. It was shortly after the new series of *Drive to Survive* had been released and for some reason I feared the worst.

'Don't tell me,' I said. 'I'm being sued by every person who has watched the new series so far.'

'Not quite,' said Stuart. 'Although it does involve something you said one day which they decided to use in one of the episodes.'

'Could it get me sacked?' I said.

'I doubt it,' said Stuart.

'OK then. Could it make me money?'

'Probably not, although it maybe should.'

Now I was confused. 'Just put me out of my misery,' I said.

Stuart started to describe the clip in question, and when he did I almost foking died. I think we were in Saudi Arabia, and as the sun beats down the camera is apparently following Stuart and me to the paddock. 'Do you want an umbrella?' he says to me. 'Fok off,' I reply. 'That would hurt my ego, standing there with somebody holding an umbrella for me.' I then say in a child's voice, 'Oh, there's a little bit of sun and I need an umbrella' – obviously implying that only idiots with big egos would ask for that. As soon as I finish talking it cuts to Otmar Szafnauer from Alpine who has got somebody holding an umbrella for him!

'Jeezoz Christ,' I said to Stuart. 'Somebody's going to come looking for me one day, you do know that. Maybe I should start hiring a bodyguard.'

Just then, Stuart went on to Google, typed something in and said, 'Here, look at this.'

'Oh my God,' I said to him. 'What the fok is that?'

'T-shirts. They're all over the internet.'

Somebody had designed a T-shirt that had my head on it with an umbrella sticking out of the top and the words UMBRELLAS HURT MY EGO written underneath. Then he showed me another one that had me wearing sunglasses with the same slogan.

'Have these people got nothing better to do?' I asked him.

'What, you mean better to do than exploiting you and making loads of money? Probably not.'

2019

THE TITLE SPONSOR

2019 was a leveller, not just for the team but for me in my role as team principal. In terms of my responsibilities the role was widening as in 2018 I had also become involved in sponsorship. When we started the team Gene had said that he would deal with that side of things, which was fine by me. I knew very little about sponsorship, although I obviously appreciated its importance. What I found slightly strange was that by 2018 we still didn't have a title sponsor in place at Haas, but as it wasn't within my remit I simply assumed that Gene was happy with us not having one. It turned out that he had actually hired somebody in the United States to find some sponsors for the team but it hadn't worked out. Then, in the autumn of 2018, a sponsorship agency got in touch with us in the UK to say that an energy drink company called Rich Energy was interested in becoming our title sponsor. 'OK,' said Gene. 'You speak to them and see what you can do.'

The reason I think this might be interesting to F1 fans, apart from the enormous amount of foking drama it caused, is that people will probably assume that Formula 1 teams have entire departments to deal with things like sponsorship. Today that's true, although you don't have to go back very far to find something more akin to what you'd see at a minor league baseball team, Haas being a case in point. As an entity within our team, though, sponsorship had basically lain dormant for the first three years of its existence so we had some catching up to do. All in all I quite enjoyed helping to bring in sponsors, partly because it involved working with people, and partly because helping to get a deal over the line benefited the team. It was pretty cool actually. Or at least some of it was.

The CEO of Rich Energy was a man called William Storey, and in October 2018 he came out to visit us at the US Grand Prix. Although none of us had ever heard of Rich Energy before, he was a pretty convincing guy so we took it to the next stage. Bearing in mind the amount of money we were asking for, which was £15 million a year, what we should have done next was hire somebody to do some serious digging on Storey and the company, but at the time we were still knee-deep in the disqualification appeal. We did get somebody to do some due diligence, however, and as far as I know it all checked out.

We ended up signing a multi-year deal with Rich Energy worth £15 million a year at the end of 2018, and in January 2019 we announced the partnership to the world at the unveiling of the new car. This took place at the RAC Club in London and I don't mind admitting that I felt a little bit out of place there. It's seriously foking posh. I also got lost several times so once I found the car and the drivers I didn't move very far.

The first time I smelled a rat with Rich Energy was when I couldn't find anybody who had ever tried the drink before. We ended up having it in the motorhome during some Grand Prix weekends but as far as I know it wasn't available in any supermarkets. In fact there were even rumours circulating before the start of the season, so I was later told, that the drink didn't exist. What makes this even stranger is that at the launch event Storey told the press that he intended Rich Energy to become the market leader and beat Red Bull 'on and off the track'. What, with an invisible foking drink? That's a big ambition.

I was later told that at the time he started talking to us Storey had already agreed a deal in principle with Williams to become their title sponsor and was supposed to have met up with Claire Williams in Austin. He had arranged to meet Claire and her representatives at a restaurant there but didn't turn up as he was talking to us. Williams went on to secure Rokit instead as their title sponsor, which I think worked out OK, so they definitely dodged a bullet. The story gets even better, though, as before they approached Williams, Rich Energy claimed to have made an offer to save the Force India team that had just gone into administration. According to ESPN, Storey was not considered a viable long-term owner of the team so Rich Energy's offer was dismissed, prompting Force India to be placed in administration. Lance Stroll then came to their rescue, repackaged the team as Racing Point, turned it into Aston Martin, and it's all been downhill ever since.

The next rat came in the form of a request from Rich Energy before the Canadian Grand Prix for us to remove part of their logo from all the branding. I later found out that this was because a company called Whyte Bikes had taken Rich Energy to court claiming that they had stolen the Whyte Bikes logo, which was a deer's head. I looked at both and they were strikingly similar. As well as ordering Rich Energy to remove the offending logo from all their branding and pay Whyte Bikes over £30,000, the judge stated that Storey had been an unreliable witness. Had I been made aware of the circumstances behind us having to remove somebody else's antlers from our livery at the time, alarm bells would have rung and I would have done something about it. As it was, I wasn't, and so we just agreed to their request.

Incidentally, the entire Rich Energy debacle became the subject of an episode of *Drive to Survive*, and having been told all about it by Stuart Morrison I have to tell you now that some of the things that are said in that episode are just bullshit, starting with a claim by Storey at the start of our relationship that he had put up a personal guarantee of £35 million. Knowing what I know now, I'm not sure he had £35, let alone £35 million.

It's safe to say that the start of the 2019 season did not go well for us, and by race nine, which was Austria, we had had just four points finishes. There were various reasons for this which I'll come on to in a moment, but on the Wednesday before race ten, which was Silverstone, Rich Energy posted a tweet claiming that they had terminated their deal with us with immediate effect due to 'poor on-track performances', as well as something about the attitude in F1 being too PC.

'I take it they haven't terminated the deal,' Stuart Morrison said to me on spotting the tweet.

'Of course not. If they had I'd have told you and we'd have prepared a statement.'

'We're probably going to have to do that anyway as the press will want to know what's going on.'

Sure enough, the press were on to us like a flash and we told them that as far as we were concerned Rich Energy were still the

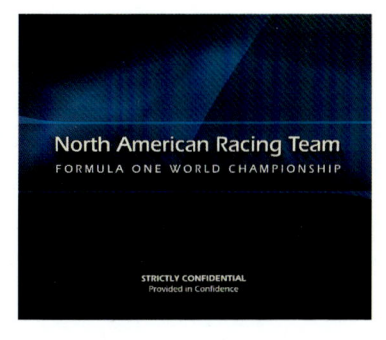

Above: The eight-page presentation I created to pitch a new Formula 1 team, then called NART.

Above: With the great Niki Lauda when we first worked together in Formula 1. Niki was a huge supporter of my dream to build a new team.

Left: A blast from the past. With Christian Horner in our younger days.

Below: Guenther the businessman. In training for my many calls to Gene.

Above: Joining the ranks of the team principals in 2016. I was more excited than I look.

Left: The moment of truth. In Barcelona for the first day of testing in 2016, the start of our debut season.

Right: Time to go racing. Celebrating with the team as we scored our first points.

Above: I soon got used to the more familiar feeling of losing, or things going horribly wrong.

Right: The team gifted me a walking stick before the race in Shanghai in 2017, for my 152nd birthday. It sure felt like it!

Below: Problem solving with Ayao Komatsu and Arron Melvin, the head of our aero department, became a familiar activity.

Above: With Toto in Austria in 2018, after scoring double points.

Above: Talking to the press. 'So, Guenther, when are you having your heart attack?'

Above: Romain emerges from the fireball in Bahrain. One of the biggest reliefs of my life.

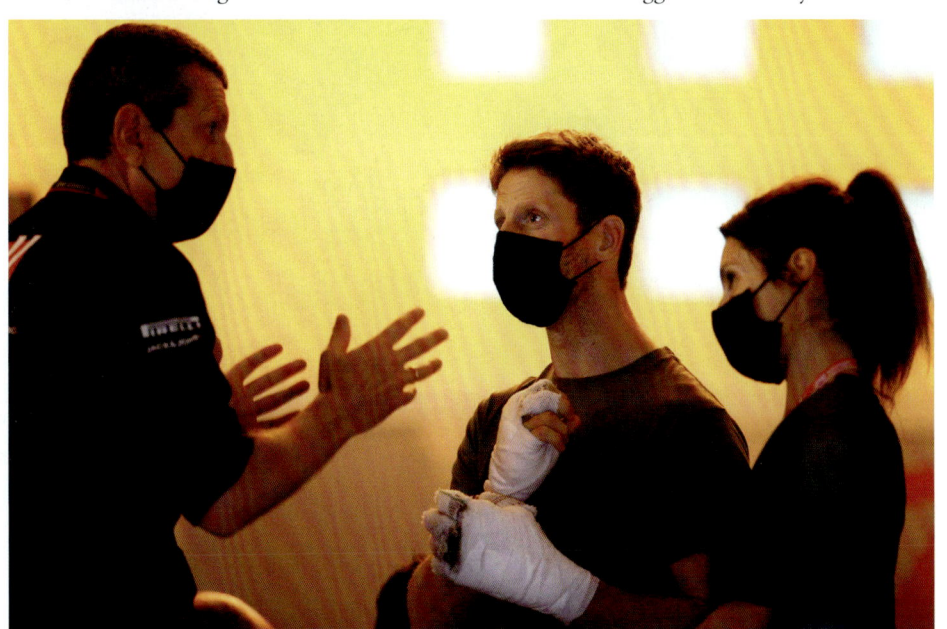

Above: Fortunately his singed hands were the worst of his injuries.

Right: Covid hits Formula 1, and the world. At least I can still express my emotions through my eyes.

Left: With the very modest Eddie Irvine in 2022.

Right: The *Drive to Survive* effect kicks in. At least the Australian fans were a little kinder about my age.

Left: Perfecting the Steiner Selfie. Always a strange experience, but I have loved meeting people all over the world.

Left: Guenther the author. My first piece of quality literature.

Above: 'Guenther, would you come with me please?' With Mohammed Ben Sulayem, president of the FIA. I always had a tense relationship with the sport's governing body.

Right: Moving up in the world. We were invited to Downing Street in 2023. I think the British government had seen how Haas coped with underperformance and figured they could learn a thing or two.

Left: Back in Melbourne in 2023. Through all of the highs and lows at Haas, I never lost sight of how lucky we were to be working in the sport we love.

Right: A moment of contemplation in Suzuka towards the end of the 2023 season. Perhaps I knew what was coming.

Below: With my wife, Gertie. She backed my dream from the beginning and stood by me every step of the way.

title sponsor of Haas F1. They'd paid the first half of the season in advance and were still in credit, although only just.

The following day the newspapers were full of it and some of the quotes from Storey were bizarre to say the least. In the *Sun* newspaper he likened our car to a milk float and then somebody – we don't know who, it might have been him – tweeted the same thing during the Grand Prix, even including a photograph of a milk float with Storey as the driver. 'What a foking weirdo,' I said when Stuart showed me this. 'This guy should be in hospital. He needs help.'

Things became a bit clearer directly after the British Grand Prix when we were informed by a board member at Rich Energy that an internal struggle was taking place and as such they apologized for what had happened. The board were keen to continue the partnership and asked us to release the following statement on their behalf:

We wholeheartedly believe in the Haas F1 Team, its performance, and the organization as a whole and we are fully committed to the current sponsorship agreement in place. We also completely believe in the product of Formula 1 and the platform it offers our brand. Clearly the rogue actions of one individual have caused great embarrassment. We are in the process of legally removing the individual from all executive responsibilities. They may speak for themselves but their views are not those of the company. We wish to confirm our commitment to the Haas F1 Team, Formula 1, and to thank the Haas F1 Team for their support and patience whilst this matter is dealt with internally.

Soon after that I became bored with all of the bullshit, and to cut a long story slightly shorter, and despite what Storey said on *Drive to Survive* which again is bullshit, we ended up terminating the agreement and so in September we removed their branding from the cars, the wagons and the motorhome and just tried to forget about them. In my opinion the whole thing was just a vanity project for a snake oil salesman and unfortunately we got duped.

In terms of how much hassle this created, working with Rich Energy was a pretty expensive lesson, but because of the things we learned it put us in good stead going forward. Also, we got £7.5 million, which wasn't too bad.

The fiasco with Rich Energy notwithstanding, the idea of having more external sponsors at Haas and me being partly responsible for negotiating and schmoozing them turned out to be the proverbial double-edged sword as it seemed like the more money we brought in, the less there was to spend. Unfortunately things were about to get a lot worse.

THE SEASON

I have already alluded to the fact that the season was pretty difficult but I suppose I had better expand on that. To be honest, I wish I didn't have to.

Testing went OK in 2019, and with the knowledge that we hadn't made as much progress in the wind tunnel as we would have liked. We also had a few reliability issues which were a worry, but by the end of the second test they had all been ironed out. Unless something is noticeably wrong with a car, drivers are usually positive after testing, and this was no exception. Kevin in particular seemed happy and said that partly due to the new regulations, which included a wider front wing and an enlarged rear wing, it was going to be easier to follow and overtake other cars.

I arrived in Melbourne on the Tuesday before the race and some time during Wednesday while I was at the track I received the awful news that Charlie Whiting had passed away. It started off as a rumour that he hadn't been very well but then after a while it was confirmed that he had died. I remember my stomach dropping when I heard the news. You know that feeling when you suddenly feel very heavy? Charlie had a unique way of being commanding without ever having to shout or swear, at least to my knowledge. He did it through being respected, and despite our disagreements nobody respected Charlie more than I did. A lot of people would probably claim the same, and I think all of us would be right, in that everybody in F1 had respect for Charlie.

I lost count of the number of times I called him during the licence application and he always answered every question for me. Also, far from just telling me what I wanted to hear all the time, if he had an issue with what I was trying to do he would tell me. Bernie might well have been the brains behind the sport during the pre-Liberty Media era, at least in terms of business, but Charlie was the heart, as was proven by the reaction from us all when he passed away. God bless Charlie Whiting. He was definitely one of the good guys.

FP1 and FP2 in Melbourne both went OK but in FP3 Romain went fourth fastest and Kevin fifth. Things got even better during qualifying when, for the third time in as many years at Melbourne, both drivers made it through to Q3. Romain ended up qualifying P6, just four tenths off Leclerc in the Ferrari, and Kevin qualified P7 ahead of Lando Norris and Kimi Räikkönen. The only downer to the session was a fine of €5,000 for an unsafe pit release. Then again, if it hadn't been a fine it would have been a grid penalty so we took it on the chin.

During the race everything went OK for us until lap thirty when Romain had to retire due to having a loose front left wheel. Yes, I'm afraid you did read that correctly. On lap fifteen he'd come in for a new set of tyres and the mechanic responsible for the front left wheel had had trouble attaching it. Once again, this was actually down to the wheel nut and not human error. Then again, it was a problem that we thought had been sorted out and we were not happy. Kevin made the end of the day slightly brighter by finishing P6, so a points finish, but the weekend was obviously overshadowed by the fact that Charlie had passed away.

By the time we left Bahrain two weeks later the first of a series of issues that ended up plaguing us in 2019 had become apparent. This one was to do with tyre management and it had us scratching our heads for pretty much the entire season. The rear tyres would overheat very easily and start sliding, which obviously affected race pace. The thing is, because we qualified well we were reluctant to admit that it might be an aero problem, which it was, and instead we tried to influence the tyre from the outside.

By the time we got to Barcelona things had gone from bad to worse but there was hope in the form of an upgrade package for Romain's car that we obviously hoped would turn things around, or at the very least point us in the right direction. After the race the result was inconclusive with regard to how well the upgrade had worked but a double points finish helped to galvanize everyone.

Eight days later, on Monday 20 May, we received more bad news. My friend of almost twenty years and my mentor in Formula 1, Niki Lauda, had passed away in a hospital in Zurich. I had known it was coming as he'd been ill for some time but it was still a big shock. The last time I talked to Niki was the day before his birthday in February. I always called him on his birthday, but as this was his seventieth I decided to call a day early to avoid the rush. Although he'd sounded ill he was still his usual self and was full of questions about how our preparations for the new season were going. It's a bit of a cliché I suppose, but Niki Lauda had Formula 1 running through his veins and I have still never met anyone with as much passion for the sport as he had.

Not only was Niki the first person to hire me in Formula 1, while I was working for him he introduced me to so many people, and boy did that make a difference. He was also my biggest supporter when I was trying to form what eventually became Haas and did everything in his power to help me make it happen. Remember that time when he came to inspect what we had done at the start of our first season? I made a bit of a joke about that earlier in the book, and although Niki was laughing (we all were) it was an inspection of sorts because he wanted to make sure that we had everything in place and had given ourselves the best chance of doing well. Not because he had a stake in the team – he did not – but because he wanted his friend and the members of the team he had put together to succeed. I still miss him.

Monaco at the end of May gave us our last points finish until Germany in July, but in the meantime a little bit of drama unfolded. That's me being sarcastic, by the way. We're back to Italian opera territory here, just with a lot more shouting and marginally less make-up.

By the time we got to Silverstone the upgrade package had still not delivered the results we had expected so in order to gather more data we decided to revert Romain's car to the factory spec it ran at Melbourne and then compare the two. We were still trying to get to the bottom of why the drivers had been struggling to heat up the tyre's bulk temperature during the race, which had been the root cause of its pace, or should I say lack of it. Once the tyres are too cold to be effective they slide, and the surface temperature shoots up which reduces their performance even further. Ever since Bahrain we had tried different set-ups, playing around with the suspension, but nothing had worked.

Also, the problems we had at one race would be different at the next, which is when we decided to compare the upgrade to the aero spec and set-up we had used in Melbourne.

Unfortunately what was supposed to have been a valuable data-collecting exercise with potentially even some points at the end of it turned out to be a disaster. During the very first lap of the race while exiting Arena, Romain and Kevin banged wheels which gave them both a puncture. As they then went through Brooklands they were passed by the rest of the field. 'What the fok are those idiots doing?' I said to Ayao Komatsu on the pit wall. He just had his head in his hands.

After managing to crawl back to the garage for a tyre change Romain rejoined the race no fewer than forty-seven seconds behind Robert Kubica who, thanks to him and Kevin, was now P19 instead of P20. He was about to move up another place though as a few seconds later Kevin pitted and then rejoined the race twenty seconds behind Romain. What a disaster.

Oh, hang on, it gets worse.

By lap three Kevin had been lapped by the entire foking field and by lap six he had retired. I forget why. Embarrassment, maybe? Three laps later he was joined by Romain, which brought to an end what had been an altogether enjoyable and productive weekend – NOT!

Unfortunately this was not the first time our two drivers had clashed on the track that season and I had already had to have words with them. There had also been a lot of moaning and complaining over the radio during race weekends about the car's performance and I was getting fed up with it. We all knew that the car wasn't as we wanted it to be and did not need reminding all the foking time. What happened at Silverstone was the final straw, and after retiring the two cars, Ayao and I went to my office and asked Romain and Kevin to join us.

Once they had sat down, I just exploded. Everything came out! I accused them of having let me and the team down, which they had by taking each other out, and basically said that if they did not like it they could fok off. Romain took it relatively well but Kevin less so and as he was leaving the office he slammed the door so hard that he smashed it. I only realized this after he had left, and boy was I pissed. I immediately went to try and find Kevin but he was nowhere to be seen. I needed to shout at somebody though and after finding his manager at the time, Jesper Carlsen, I laid into him big time. This of course resulted in me saying those words that, thanks to Netflix's ever-present microphones, became a kind of catchphrase for me. More than anything I think it demonstrates my unique grasp of the English language.

With the benefit of hindsight, I am now a little bit more sympathetic to why the drivers behaved like they did than I was at the time, although I have never told them that. The main reason was frustration of course, which had been present from the start of the season and was then compounded when the upgrade did not work. It was a frustrating time for everybody though, not just the drivers. The rivalry between the two, which had never been too apparent before, probably came about because the mood in the team was quite low and they ended up taking their frustrations out on each other. That's just a theory. Either way, none of it was very healthy.

To sum up just how crazy 2019 was for Haas, at the race after Silverstone, the German GP, we ended up having our second (and unfortunately last) double points finish of the season. I know, how foking mad is that? The weekend started off badly when Kevin had to be towed back to the garage during FP1 with a sensor failure. Still reeling from what had happened at Silverstone, I remember feeling pretty dejected by this. We just couldn't get a break. By the end of qualifying my mood had improved slightly as Romain managed to get through to Q3 and qualify P6. Kevin, who qualified P12, missed out on Q3 by less than three hundredths of a second. The race was affected by heavy rain and there were six retirements and at least four safety cars. Our boys originally finished P9 and P10 which we were more than happy with, but then Antonio Giovinazzi and Kimi Räikkönen each received a thirty-second penalty which made it P7 and P8.

Apart from Kevin finishing P9 in Russia that was it with regard to points and we ended up finishing ninth in the Constructors' Championship in front of Williams. After Germany we'd been level-pegging with Alfa Romeo but they had five points finishes to our one post-Hockenheim and finished on fifty-seven points to our twenty-eight.

As well as being a leveller for the team, 2019 saw the beginning of a change in my relationship with Gene. The more 2019 failed to match 2018 the more disgruntled he became, and the more disgruntled he became the more disparaging he was about the team. After a while this really started to piss me off, and some time during the Mexico weekend at the end of October it all came to a head.

Gene had called a meeting and, as expected, instead of saying anything constructive he started complaining about the results and laying into the team. According to him, everyone was doing a shit job, including me. Honestly, the way he made it sound, it was like we'd had nothing but retirements for both cars since day one. 'But this is the nature of racing,' I said to him. 'For fok's sake, Gene, you should know that. All you're doing is making me feel bad and I don't need any help in that department at the moment.' And this is what I don't understand. Gene had been racing in NASCAR since 2002 and it had taken the team years to have any success. We, on the other hand, had tasted success at the first race. Why were we any different to NASCAR, or was this how he treated everybody? I had no idea.

Once again with the benefit of hindsight, what I perhaps should have done during the 2019 season was to turn round and say to Gene, 'OK, it's your team, if you think we're all shit you can come and run it.' Unfortunately I am not that kind of person. If a problem ever arises, especially when I'm in charge of something, I will always try and find a solution. That's not to say that I won't accept help of course, providing it is offered to me. One thing I won't do, however, is start grovelling for it.

Regardless of what Gene said or wanted to believe, one thing I had to try and do was keep all this in perspective, which is easier said than done when the owner of the team is telling you that you're doing shit. The truth is, though, that in our first four years on the grid Haas had had two very promising seasons and one extremely good one, and as I have said more than once during this section, 2019 was a leveller.

2020

THE PANDEMIC

I can't remember when I first heard about Covid, or coronavirus as I think it was called at first. It was probably on the news or something. Then again, I generally try and avoid the news as it's always so depressing. Now I come to think of it, I'm pretty sure it was Gertie who told me. She usually tells me everything I need to know that isn't about Formula 1. I don't remember being too worried about it though, at least at first. I never tend to worry about things I cannot affect, and dealing with a potential global pandemic was not within my skillset. One thing I do remember is the growing sense of unease that seemed to be engulfing the world at the time, but like most people I just kept my head down and carried on carrying on.

The first thing we did after the 2019 season was over was decide on the team colours for the new livery, as well as everything else. The original idea was to revert to using red, black and grey, which had been the team colours prior to 2019, but somebody suggested swapping the grey for white, which we went with. Boy, did that feel good. Although it was only aesthetic, not having a black car with gold lettering helped to exorcize a few unpleasant demons regarding certain incidents and people. To be honest, I was never especially fond of having a grey car either so when somebody showed me the livery for the VF-20 I was really pleased. It looked shit hot.

Over the winter we developed the car in the wind tunnel and Ferrari provided us with a new gear box and suspension, as usual. We had to stick with the same concept so a lot of the development time in the wind tunnel was spent ironing out the tyre issue, which we now knew for sure was aerodynamic. All in all the design guys were happy with the progress they made and by the time it came to testing we were allowing ourselves to smile sometimes and even utter words of confidence to each other.

Going into the off season after a bad one is obviously a relief as it gives you time to regroup and improve things. It's different after a good one, of course, as you never want it to end. The worst situation is when you have shown improvement towards the end of a season as you want to see how long that can carry on for. As disappointing as 2019 was, there had also been many positives with the car which we never got to appreciate because of the tyre issue. So, if the design guys had managed to solve the problem we might well have a good car on our hands. That's what we all hoped.

As usual, we were the first team to release a rendering of our new livery and the response from the public was just as it had been from the team, overwhelmingly positive, with many people saying that it was the best-looking we had produced so far. Despite it only being an aesthetic, to receive some positive feedback like that so early is always good, especially when things have been difficult. Sponsor-wise, we hadn't yet found a replacement. Several agencies were working on our behalf but given what we'd experienced last time we were going to have to be very careful.

By the time I landed in Barcelona for pre-season testing on 17 February things had ramped up a few gears with regard to the virus, and regardless of where you were or who you were with, it was the main point of conversation. This in itself felt very strange as it was an obvious distraction from what we were there to do. Then again, how do you ignore an impending global pandemic? Various measures were being introduced in countries around the world to try and stop the spread of the disease although nothing had been introduced in Spain at the time. The atmosphere at the test was different though, I remember that. Although some of the people there are often a bit bleary-eyed as they've basically just come out of hibernation, weirdos like me who never stop have been dying to get back to a track for months so there's usually an air of excitement. That was definitely less noticeable this year, with good reason.

Testing went OK, although as always we would have appreciated a few more days of it. You know, ten or twenty maybe. The first test in Barcelona was a bit of a struggle and we had a lot of bad luck. Water leaks, punctures – it wasn't good. Out of the three days at the first test we probably only managed a day and a half of testing in all so we just had to hope for more at the second test. That went marginally better and we came away with a lot of data having had fewer issues.

The ten days in between us leaving Barcelona after testing and then landing in Melbourne for the Australian Grand Prix were like living in the Twilight Zone. By this time nobody was talking about anything other than this new virus and the F1 rumour mill was in full flow. I remember somebody telling me just after we landed in Melbourne that a Premier League soccer match had been postponed as a precautionary measure and that several players had been forced to self-isolate.

The thing is, I recall reading statements from the UK government a day or two before in Banbury saying that in their opinion there was no reason to cancel anything. Although I hate the foking term as it is usually a sign that people don't know what they're talking about, this was indeed a 'fluid situation' as things were changing almost by the hour. In fact, there is no better demonstration of this than the decision to go ahead and move the entire F1 circus, which comprises many thousands of tonnes of equipment, halfway across the world to Australia to put on a Grand Prix. It was obviously taken because the powers that be thought it would be possible, yet with the benefit of hindsight there was no way it was ever going to happen. That's how fast things were moving at the time.

On 11 March, so four days before the race was due to take place, four members of the Haas Team started displaying the symptoms of Covid and were immediately put into isolation. Later on they were tested and fortunately came back negative, but because Melbourne only had one facility that was capable of testing for the virus and could only handle five hundred cases at a time, it took an age for the results to come back. And it wasn't just Haas who were interested in whether they were positive. The entire sport was waiting on tenterhooks.

At about the same time a McLaren Team member also started displaying symptoms, and after being isolated and then tested they eventually came back positive. This person, as far as we knew, was the first member of the travelling F1 circus to test positive for Covid, and as a result of this McLaren decided to withdraw from the race.

All of this happened on the back of some pretty damning criticism of the governing body from the two most decorated and respected drivers on the grid, Lewis Hamilton and Sebastian Vettel. They were both furious that while the rest of the world had started taking precautions against the spread of Covid and were practising social distancing and avoiding mass gatherings, F1 were still talking about getting several hundred thousand people together at a race track for an entire weekend.

'I am really very, very surprised that we are here,' Lewis said at a press conference. 'I think it's really shocking that we are all sitting in this room. There are so many fans here today and it seems like the rest of the world is reacting, probably a little bit late, yet Formula 1 continues to go on.' Later on, when asked why he thought the Grand Prix was still going ahead, Lewis said simply, 'Cash is king. I can't add much more to it. I don't feel like I should shy away from my opinion.'

Sebastian went one step further by insisting that should there be any fatalities associated with F1, the drivers would act collectively and simply refuse to race. 'We hope it doesn't get that far,' Seb said. 'We [the drivers] share a common opinion on big decisions and that would qualify as a very big decision. Ultimately, as I said before, you look at yourself and I think we would be mature enough to look after ourselves and pull the handbrake in that case.'

One day later, on Thursday 12 March, the FIA, F1, the promoters and the Melbourne health authorities called a press conference at Albert Park to announce to the world that the race was cancelled. We had been told this a few hours before at a meeting between the team principals and the FIA so had been expecting it. What was surprising, as Lewis had said, was that it had taken so long to sort out. On waking up that morning one of the team back in Banbury had messaged me to say that apparently the UK government were about to ban all but essential travel in the UK and ask people to work from home. Over in the United States too they were introducing all kinds of measures, yet here we all were.

The prevailing mood within the F1 camp once the Grand Prix had been cancelled was to get out of Australia as soon as possible and get home to our families. There was also an element of fear as we had no idea whether the airports we were hoping to fly into would still be open, let alone the airspace of the countries we were flying into and over. Also, the people involved in the F1 circus number in their thousands so the logistics for us alone were going to be a nightmare. I'm not sure how they managed to do it but fortunately we were all able to leave Australia pretty quickly, and about forty hours after doing so I was safely at home in North Carolina with Gertie and Greta.

THE FALLOUT

As soon as we'd all had time to catch our breath we opened up the lines of communication and started talking about what might or might not happen next. F1 Commission meetings took place regularly online but during the days and weeks after Melbourne my phone hardly stopped ringing. The reality that F1 might not be able to stage some or perhaps any of the forthcoming races in 2020 had already started to hit home, as had the possibility that some of the teams might even go to the wall as a result.

The Chinese Grand Prix had been cancelled before we even arrived in Melbourne so by the time we left Australia we were already two races down. As the days went on more and more races were called off. Soon after Australia the inaugural Vietnamese Grand Prix was cancelled, which they had been planning for several years. Then Bahrain went, and then after that the Dutch and Spanish Grands Prix.

I don't know if you remember, but there were a lot of false dawns during the early weeks of Covid and barely a day went by without me being made aware of a rumour or an article online (written by Mickey Mouse) saying that a certain Grand Prix would be the first one to go ahead. I suppose that was understandable given that we all needed hope, but most of these stories were bullshit, not least the one I read a few days after Australia suggesting that Monaco might be the first race of the 2020 season to go ahead. Monaco? It would be easier to socially distance in a foking telephone box, with or without the general public there. I almost spat out my espresso when I read that. Funnily enough, the day after that Monaco was cancelled, which for many fans was when the enormity of what was happening hit home. No Monaco Grand Prix? That felt weird.

Over the next couple of weeks Canada, Azerbaijan and then France all announced that their races would not go ahead in 2020, which wiped out the entire calendar until the end of June. On paper this obviously looked like an unmitigated disaster. Hundreds of millions of dollars had already been lost in revenue, not just to the sport and the teams but to the countless businesses that supplied the F1 circus and the external members of staff who were engaged when a Grand Prix came to town. Fortunately, instead of throwing in the towel and just capitulating, F1 and the FIA decided to carry on fighting and rather than just shutting up shop and waiting for it all to pass, which from a financial point of view must have been tempting as they could easily have curtailed some of the losses there and then, they carried on investing, planning and even innovating.

It was a huge gamble, but the attitude of F1 and the FIA was that when society was eventually allowed to come up for air again, Formula 1 had to be ready to put on a show anywhere in the world (or wherever it was allowed), start entertaining its public again and recoup some of the losses the sport had already incurred. Luckily, Formula 1 is an industry that has always thrived on complex problems and logistical and organizational challenges, and when everyone started putting their heads together we began to see a way forward.

At Haas, things became dire pretty quickly and if it hadn't been for the furlough scheme in the UK which paid people 80 per cent of their wages we would have gone to the wall almost immediately, along with thousands of other companies around the country. In Italy things weren't so straightforward and unfortunately we ended up having to let some people go. We also had to renegotiate all of our supplier contracts in the UK and in Italy to save money and just keep things ticking over.

In my role as team principal this was quite a challenging time. I was used to team members being pissed off about the fact that we'd had a shit weekend or something, but not about the fact that they might not have a job to go back to, or even a sport. What I had to keep on reminding myself and the team was that, compared to millions of other people around the world, we were actually OK. Regardless of how precarious things were, we were still employed, we were still getting paid and we still had each other. We also still had hope, which carried a very high value at the time.

Because I took part in many of the meetings about resurrecting F1, and because I had faith in Formula One Group's Chase Carey and Ross Brawn, and in Jean Todt at the FIA, I had no doubt at all that the sport would bounce back once the restrictions had been lifted. Relaying that to the team was easy, although making them believe it, or rather believe it fully, was less so. Under the circumstances that was probably the best I could hope for.

One of the most seismic moves by F1 and the FIA with regard to the survival of the teams took place in May when they announced to the world a reduction in the 2021 budget cap from $175 million per team to $145 million. The other big announcement from that particular meeting was a brand-new sliding scale for aerodynamic development, also coming in for 2021, meaning that the lower a team finished in the Constructors' Championship the more wind tunnel time it would be allowed the following year.

The people who pushed hardest for the above were McLaren's Zak Brown, Fred Vasseur who was at Alfa Romeo at the time, and me, our main argument being that if they didn't reduce the budget cap and make other changes our teams could not survive. And that wasn't bullshit, it was the truth. It wasn't plain sailing though. The three of us were not a majority and we had to come up with suggestions that would work for everyone, not just the smaller teams.

One of the most positive things to come from these efforts to keep the sport we all loved afloat and have it ready to be brought back to life at a moment's notice was the way that everyone pulled together and worked as one. For as long as was necessary all of the usual politics and sniping was put to one side and we morphed into a cohesive, determined and very capable team. It was pretty impressive actually, and I for one feel proud to have been part of it. Whether it's in the middle of a pandemic or not, the sport of Formula 1 is greater than the sum of its parts, and a reminder of that, and of what we were capable of, did us no harm whatsoever.

The upshot was that when the restrictions eventually did begin to lift in June we were ready to go and F1 already had a revised calendar in place featuring seventeen races, starting with a double-header in Austria. Given just the logistics involved versus the challenges that still lay ahead, that was an unbelievable achievement. The only compromise, apart from the fact that the race weekends had to be shortened to three days, was that everything had to take place behind closed doors, which meant no fans. The only consolation was that they could still watch the races at home. It wasn't ideal but it was better than nothing.

The overwhelming emotion that I think everyone must have been feeling when the news came through about the restart was relief. We couldn't have cared less that we'd have to wear masks at the tracks, get tested ten times a day and live in bubbles. We were back doing what we loved best. What's more, thanks to the efforts I have already mentioned, F1 was the first major sport in the world to re-emerge from Covid and start competing again once the restrictions were lifted, which is once again a testament to its capability.

Forza F1!

THE RESHUFFLE

As much as the team and I were looking forward to going racing again after lockdown there was one issue that for some time had been stifling my excitement and anticipation. Although the teams had obviously had to make cutbacks at the start of the pandemic, because of its intention as a sport to return as soon as possible with all guns blazing the majority of F1 teams continued to invest money and develop their cars. Well, all but one of the teams. Not only did Haas lay people off in Italy but we also mothballed the wind tunnel, so in addition to not modifying the current car at all we did no development work whatsoever, either for this season or the following.

Unfortunately, unlike the other team owners, Gene decided not to back either the sport or his team during this period and did not want to spend any money at all while the pandemic was still at its height. Once again, as the owner of the team this was his prerogative, but from my own point of view it was devastating, not just because I knew that we would not be competitive if and when we started racing again but because I also knew what it would do to the team. Foregone conclusions are bad for sport no matter what, but knowing for sure that you're going to finish last is pretty hard to take.

As usual, this was something I could not talk about publicly as if I had it could have caused trouble. Also, the longer things went on the less confidence and enthusiasm Gene seemed to have for the sport (despite the fact that we were always moving closer to racing again), and the last thing I wanted to do was antagonize him. After all, he had mothballed the wind tunnel. What if the team was next?

Having discussed this with two friends of mine recently, each of them turned round and said something along the lines of, 'Well, couldn't he have just sold the team?' What, during a pandemic? It wasn't like today when F1 teams are worth a fortune. As it was, in addition to me being part of the efforts to have F1 ready to be resurrected as and when, I ended up spending much of the first half of 2020 trying to persuade Gene not to close the team down. It was a burden that I don't mind admitting weighed heavily on my shoulders and is one of the few occasions when the job of team principal kept me awake at night.

By far the most perilous time during this period was when the new Concorde Agreement – the contract between Formula 1, the FIA and the teams – which would come into play from 2021 onwards needed to be signed. Because of the sport's precarious situation Gene had let it be known that he wasn't keen on investing more money in the team and so being asked to sign the agreement, which at the end of the day was all about ensuring the future of the sport, would ultimately force his hand. If he didn't sign I knew we would be finished as he'd want out, but if he did . . . well, at least the team would still be alive.

One thing I knew for sure at this point was that even if Gene did decide to sign the agreement, with the absence of any investment or development we would not be in a position to compete at any level for at least the next two seasons, and in 2021 we would almost certainly be at the back of the grid. Can you imagine how demoralizing a prospect like that is to a team principal? It went against everything I had ever worked for in motorsport.

Gene eventually said that he would sign the Concorde Agreement and it was finally signed in August 2020. I needed to find enough sponsorship money and make enough cuts to ensure that he didn't need to invest anything in 2021, otherwise it would not work commercially. Given my experiences so far with sponsorship I did not relish the challenge, but what choice did I have? Also, making further cuts when we were already running things on a shoestring was not going to be easy.

The only obvious substantial saving we could make for the following season was to change drivers. Both Kevin and Romain's contracts were up for renewal at the end of 2020 and so after discussing it with Gene we agreed to make a change, not only because it would save the team money but because I was fairly sure that neither Kevin nor Romain would want to drive an uncompetitive car for two seasons, let alone one. I obviously did not know for sure how uncompetitive the car was going to be in 2020, but 2021 would be a certainty. Despite this, and despite the logic of them both moving on, I was not looking forward to having the conversation. But it had to be done.

Both drivers took the news as well as could be expected and there were no arguments or even raised voices. They appreciated how demoralizing it would be to drive an uncompetitive car and how damaging that might be to their careers. It wouldn't be much of a showcase.

I should point out that I could only tell the drivers and the team so much about what was going on financially. As my boss and the owner of the team, I still had a loyalty to Gene. Also, there are two sides to every story and Gene might well have had reasons for what he did. Fortunately, at least with regard to this situation, just about every team was experiencing some kind of financial issue at the time which prevented people from asking too many questions.

From the team's point of view, the financial opportunity presented by letting Romain and Kevin go went beyond just saving our two biggest salaries. Ferrari had an academy driver called Mick Schumacher (son of Michael, of course) who, if and when it started, would be competing in the 2020 Formula 2 Championship and who Ferrari were keen on putting in an F1 car next season, although not one of their own, at least for now. For agreeing to take on Mick, the Scuderia were willing to pay the team an amount of money which would go towards his wages.

The second opportunity arose after speaking to Chase Carey. After Gene's ultimatum he was one of the first people I consulted, and when I explained my predicament he put me in touch with several companies that he knew were looking to get into F1 including a very large Russian fertilizer company called Uralkali. To cut a long story short, the owner of Uralkali, Dmitry Mazepin, had a son called Nikita who would be competing against Mick in the Formula 2 Championship and he had exactly the same ambitions for Nikita as Ferrari had for Mick. What's more, the amount of money Dmitry was willing to invest in the team would allow us to carry on operating. Just as importantly, we could start developing a new and hopefully competitive car for 2022. It was the perfect solution to a shit situation.

Having to tell Romain and Kevin that their services would not be needed for 2021 before the 2020 season had even begun was pretty shit. I knew more than anybody just how much they enjoyed being part of the team and not being able to keep them on and provide them with a car that would do justice to their talents hurt me a lot. Once again, this went against everything I had worked for in the industry, and the only reason I was still doing it, apart from wanting to keep the team together, was because the situation itself was so unprecedented. I had no idea what was going to happen long term – nobody did – but something inside me wanted to stay and find out.

THE RESTART

There aren't many things in life more satisfying than relaying good news to people you care about, and being able to tell the team and then Gertie and Greta that we were finally going to start racing in July is up there with the best. In fact, the only one that can rival that is when I called Gene and then Gertie to tell them that we'd scored points at our first race.

When the news broke, everyone was obviously delighted. I remember feeling so relieved but at the same time excited. One thing I didn't even think about at the time was how competitive or uncompetitive we might be. Based on the fact that the other teams had carried on developing and investing I kind of knew what the answer would be. Then again, the team was still together — just — Formula 1 was very much alive and we were about to go racing for the first time in eight months. Life was actually pretty good.

Turning up in Spielberg for the Austrian double-header without any fans was just as we had predicted, a bit foking weird. But there was nothing we could do about it and, as you now know, I do not waste my time worrying about things that I have no control over. There were positives to this, such as being able to move more freely around the circuit, but as I keep saying, I am a people person so I would take fans over freedom every time. What I also found a bit eerie at first was the lack of noise around the circuit, and I couldn't shake that feeling even when the cars were on the track. As well as having one of the biggest audience capacities on the calendar at around a hundred thousand, the Red Bull Ring is an undulating circuit and the fans in the stands form part of the landscape. As such, we really missed having them there.

The reality of how good the car was and where we might be in comparison to the other teams started to become apparent almost immediately when in qualifying Kevin and Romain lined up P16 and P17 respectively. Then, during the race, while both were running just outside the points, they suffered braking issues and were forced to retire. The only positive from the race was that both drivers said that, despite the problem with the brakes, the car was potentially raceable. Had we been able to carry on developing it this would have been good news, but our hands were tied.

At race two of the double-header, which was named the Styrian Grand Prix (Styria being the name of the province where the track is situated), we fared better. Both cars managed to finish, thank God, and we ended the race just outside the points with Kevin P12 and Romain P13. Although this was promising we had to manage our expectations. What we had in our favour, however, was a highly motivated team who were aware of our situation and who were willing to do anything they could in order to try and compensate for the lack of development. In real terms we would probably have to rely on either luck or strategy for any gains, but that was OK.

In Hungary, race three, this paid dividends by way of a very brave decision that was made during the formation lap. Wet weather prior to the start of the race prompted the grid to line up on intermediates (except Kevin, who started on wets), but at the end of the formation lap both our cars came in and switched to mediums. Although this meant that Kevin and Romain started the race from the pit lane, within a few laps Kevin was up to P3 and Romain P4. Things obviously changed once the other cars had pitted but after managing his tyres well Kevin finished the race P9 while Romain finished P15 but drove well. Unfortunately, Kevin was handed a ten-second penalty after the race (from memory it was something to do with communications during the formation lap) but it still gave him tenth which meant a point.

Despite everyone's best efforts to keep the sport completely Covid-free, given the number of people that comprised the F1 community it was inevitable that at some point somebody would test positive. We came away from Austria without a single case, which is astonishing when you think about it, but during the Hungarian Grand Prix weekend two people tested positive. They had not been present in Austria and were isolated immediately, but it brought home just how susceptible the sport was. Then again, two positive tests after three Grands Prix in two different countries wasn't a bad record.

Instead of being able to push on from Hungary and establish a place in the midfield, which is what we had been hoping for pre-Covid, we started finishing races at the back alongside Alfa Romeo and Williams. Like it or not, that was where we belonged for the time being and we had no option but to keep our heads down, carry on fighting and keep hoping for opportunities like the one that materialized in Hungary. As the other teams carried on developing and introducing upgrades the gap became wider, and with very little luck and next to no strategic opportunities in the offing, by the time we got to Turkey – race fourteen, in mid-November – we had just three points to our name.

The next race was Bahrain, which over the years had been a fairly happy hunting ground for us. Then again, we were all a little bit tired by this point. Not just physically tired, but tired of the fact that our definition of success had gone from being a double points finish or qualifying on the third row of the grid to one of our drivers scraping into Q2 and the other not retiring. I could not let this show under any circumstances, either to the media or the team. The team were all aware what was happening but I just had to keep on reminding them that there was light at the end of the tunnel. If only it hadn't been so far away!

Our qualifying results post-Hungary had been as uninspiring as our race results, and in Bahrain we continued the trend by lining up P18 and P19 on the grid. The only car that was potentially worse than ours in 2020 was the Williams. Then again, without wanting to be disrespectful to Nicholas Latifi, if the team had had somebody of George Russell's calibre driving both their cars they might well have given us a run for our money. That's how bad things had become.

The start of the race went without incident, and by turn two Romain had managed to gain two places and Kevin one. The camera angle at this point was an aerial shot which makes it harder to identify the cars, and a few seconds later as they were passing through turn three one of the midfield cars suddenly veered off the track and went straight into the barrier before bursting into flames. In all my years in motorsport I had never seen anything like it before. It was an inferno. I didn't know who the driver was but my immediate thought was that they must have died instantly.

The next shot on the screen in front of me showed that the car had split completely in two. The front half, which included the cockpit, had disappeared through the barrier and was behind a wall of flames while the rear half was in vision and to the left of the inferno. Despite the scene in front of me, my eyes fixed on just one thing. The colour of what remained of the car was white, and on it was some red lettering. It was one of ours.

In an effort to gain another place, Romain had clipped Daniil Kvyat's Alpha Tauri which had caused him to ricochet into the barrier. He'd been travelling at around 145mph at the time of impact and was carrying about 100kg of fuel, hence the fireball.

'Who is it?' I asked Ayao.

'It's Romain.'

By now the TV director was switching from a camera in a helicopter that was hovering almost directly above the scene of the crash to one that was situated on the other side of the track opposite the scene of the accident. I watched the screen intently, praying for some sign of life, but there was nothing. All I could see was the rear half of a car, a mutilated barrier and a lot of flames. The aerial shot was by far the most harrowing as you couldn't even see the front half of the car. Some stewards arrived on the scene with fire extinguishers but the flames were too strong for them to make much of a difference. I'd been in motorsport long enough to know that if Romain didn't emerge very soon my original fears would be proved correct. I just couldn't see how anyone could survive something like that.

The eerie air of silence I mentioned earlier with having no

fans at the circuit was nothing compared to this. The cars were still moving but at a snail's pace and were on their way into the pits. Nobody in the pit lane said a word. Everybody just looked at the screens and prayed for good news.

As I sat there staring at the screen my brain kicked into gear and I immediately asked for silence over the team radio. Whatever we said now would be broadcast to the entire world, and for the sake of the people watching, and in particular Romain's family, it was better that we said nothing.

After what was apparently no more than half a minute but felt more like an hour I started to see some movement from the other side of the barrier. The inferno was still raging but after a few seconds I could see that it was Romain.

'It's him, he's out!' said Ayao.

Romain was out of the car but not the inferno, and he was still behind the barrier. Fortunately, as the flames continued to engulf him, one of the medical team sprayed a fire extinguisher directly at Romain while another helped him to climb over the barrier. It was an incredible act of bravery. Those guys are heroes.

I didn't know for sure but Romain seemed to be OK so my thoughts turned to his family. I had no idea if they had been watching the race or not but we had to let them know as soon as possible that he was out of the car. After getting word to them we informed Jean Todt, who is a good friend of Romain's, and then we set about letting the rest of the world know.

As soon as I was satisfied that the news was getting out there I started to make enquiries about how Romain actually was. According to one of the medical officers he had insisted on walking to the ambulance in order to let the people watching know that he was OK and had then been taken to the nearest hospital. His injuries were also not life-threatening. In fact Romain had complained only of having burned hands.

The only time I had ever experienced anything close to watching Romain's crash was in my rally days when in October 2000, during the ninth stage of the tour of Corsica, Colin McRae clipped the inside of a fast left-hand bend and plunged about 15 metres into a river, landing roof-first. While his co-driver Nicky Grist managed to scramble to safety, Colin was knocked unconscious and was trapped in the car. Although I did not see the crash (nobody did), simply because of the speed they were travelling I feared the worst, and when Colin was found by the stewards they assumed he was dead. Fortunately that wasn't the case (he'd suffered a fractured cheekbone and a bruised lung), although it took the fire brigade almost half an hour to cut him free. Thinking that somebody might have died in a crash is a lot different from seeing them at the scene and believing that they have. That too was a pretty traumatic day.

In the evening I went to visit Romain in hospital. Instead of taking flowers and grapes and crying at the foot of his bed I just sat there taking the piss out of him and called him a foking idiot. What else did you expect? All things considered he was in very good spirits, even when I was there. He certainly wouldn't be racing for a while but the burns to his hands were not serious.

There are two things that saved Romain's life that day: the halo, which protected him on impact and when the front half of the car went through the barrier, and the fire-resistant clothing, which obviously protected him from the inferno. The clothing had only just been introduced and increased protection by 20 per cent. But it was the halo that ultimately saved his life as without it he would have died instantly. Like me and so many others, Romain had also been a naysayer when the halo was first introduced. This was conclusive proof that we had all been in the wrong and that Jean Todt and the FIA had made the right decision.

The next race was the second of a Bahrain double-header called the Sakhir Grand Prix. With Romain still languishing in a hospital bed pretending to be ill we brought in our reserve driver, Pietro Fittipaldi. Pietro, who is still with the team and is the grandson of Emerson Fittipaldi, had been hired at the start of the year and he had worked hard and fitted in well. In addition to racing here in the penultimate race of the season he would also fill in for Romain in Abu Dhabi.

Incidentally, the Bahrain Grand Prix had eventually restarted and was won by Lewis, who had long since had the Championship sewn up. Kevin could only manage P17, and the final two races produced similar results for both him and Pietro. Feelings of disappointment and frustration are commonplace in motorsport and can be hard to handle sometimes, especially over a prolonged period of time. They are nothing, though, compared to the anguish and desperation you feel when a driver crashes and is feared injured or dead. All of a sudden everything is put into perspective. The former is about sport and competition and is ultimately why we are here, but the latter is about human life. In my mind there is no comparison.

In addition to watching a mad Frenchman snap a very expensive car in half while failing to score points in the Middle East, the last quarter of the year was spent putting the finishing touches to the Uralkali deal. Contrary perhaps to what became popular belief, dealing with Uralkali was fine at the beginning and the negotiations went very well. Dmitry Mazepin was straightforward, honest and fair. In fact we couldn't have asked for more from a sponsor. I have since heard dozens of horror stories about dealing with Russian businesses but I can only go by my own experience. What I had heard at the time were stories about sponsors who invest purely to get their child a drive and then feel some sort of ownership over team decisions. Our deal had similar origins of course, and I just had to pray that Dmitry and Nikita would be an exception.

Nikita Mazepin and Mick Schumacher were named as the replacements for Kevin and Romain at the beginning of December 2020. Approximately one week later Nikita posted a video of himself on his Instagram page groping a young woman in the back of a car. One minute we had a new driver line-up consisting of two promising former F2 competitors and the next we had one promising former F2 competitor and a Russian sex pest. As if the year couldn't get any more screwed up.

'Haas F1 Team does not condone the behaviour of Nikita Mazepin in the video recently posted on his social media,' we said in a statement. 'Additionally, the very fact that the video was posted on social media is also abhorrent to Haas F1 Team. The matter is being dealt with internally and no further comment shall be made at this time.'

I cannot begin to tell you how foking pissed I was about this. Not only because it was stupid and the wrong thing to do, but because we had just announced his entry into the world's highest class of international racing for open-wheel single-seater formula cars. Had he been an existing F1 driver I would have fired him from a foking cannon.

After much deliberation between ourselves and with Nikita's father, who was totally pissed with him too, we decided to give him another chance and announced it as soon as possible in the hope that by the time the 2021 season started the whole story might have died down. It was a first offence, but as far as I and the team were concerned he was already on a warning. This, by the way, was in addition to the fact that Nikita had already accrued eleven penalty points on his licence for a variety of offences, leaving him one short of an automatic ban.

Would all this be an omen for what was to come next season?

What the fok do you think.

PIT STOP

TAKING POSITIVES FROM A PANDEMIC

It wasn't just Liberty Media's bottomless pit of dollars and their endeavours online that dragged Formula 1 kicking and screaming into the twenty-first century. There were two other things that helped too: Covid and *Drive to Survive*. I appreciate that Covid was tragic for many millions of people but like most things that happen in the world, you can usually find a positive somewhere.

By the time the lockdowns started in early 2020 *Drive to Survive* had been in existence for about a year. In that time it had been popular, but it hadn't set the world on fire. Then, when Covid came along and half the world was obliged to stay indoors, people started looking for things to watch on TV and, so I've been told, a lot of them started watching *Drive to Survive*.

Something that helped to maintain and then consolidate the momentum that had been created by *Drive to Survive* was the fact that F1 was one of the first sports to start up again once the Covid restrictions were lifted, which meant that existing F1 fans could get their fix and fans who had been introduced to the sport by *Drive to Survive* could see in real time what all the fuss was about. Starting up so early was a really important move by the guys at the top, and in turn it obviously helped to maintain interest in the show. What might have happened had Covid not reared its ugly head I have no idea, but the change in demographic to the F1 audience after things had normalized was off the scale.

Pre-*Drive to Survive* and Covid, on the few occasions when people stopped me at a track during a Grand Prix (it *never* happened at other times) they were almost invariably middle-aged men. Post-Covid it was a complete cross-section of society, or at least it seemed to be. I know some of the purists like to claim that the audience *Drive to Survive* created are all armchair supporters who are here today and gone tomorrow, but that's just bullshit. Their interest might be on a different level to these guys, in that they're excited by different aspects, but that doesn't make them any less worthy or important. I have attended every day of every Grand Prix weekend for the last eight years and, believe me, the new kids on the block are as passionate about the sport, not to mention the people who are involved in the sport, as anyone I met beforehand.

The very first time I realized that something might be happening from a personal point of view as a result of *Drive to Survive* was a couple of days after the first episode of the first series went live in March 2019. I had to attend an F1 Commission meeting before the start of the season, which I was really looking forward to as they are always incredibly exciting and interesting, and as soon as I walked into the room everybody there – the other team principals, the CEO of F1, the president of the FIA – looked at me, stopped whatever they were saying, and started talking about the show.

'What the fok's the matter with everyone?' I said to Chase Carey.

'Haven't you seen it?' he said to me.

'What, *Drive to Survive*? No, I have a foking life, you know.'

'I think you should,' he said. 'You might like it. It's cool.'

As everybody talked, they kept on looking over at me, and that's when I decided that I shouldn't watch it. Whatever they were thinking, I didn't want to know. When I left the meeting I tried to forget all about *Drive to Survive* and for a few days I just about managed it. I was up to my ears in preparing for the new season at the time so wasn't paying much attention to the outside world. Then, on Tuesday 12 March, I boarded a flight from LA to Melbourne for the first race of the season, which was when I started to appreciate that there were people in the world I'd never met before who seemed to know me, or at least seemed to know who I was. The plane was full of people who were travelling to the Grand Prix and during the flight, which was about sixteen hours, I must have had at least twenty conversations with complete strangers about the previous season. It was crazy. Interesting, but crazy.

By far the most stark realization of the change in demographic that has occurred since Covid and *Drive to Survive* hit me when I turned up for a signing session on the day that *Surviving to Drive* was published in April 2023. The signing session took place at Waterstones bookshop on Piccadilly in central London at 6 p.m., and earlier that day I'd received a telephone call from Henry Vines, the publisher, to say that every ticket for the event had been sold. 'Jeezoz Christ,' I said. 'There are a lot of sick people in London these days.' Secretly I was quite relieved as I'd been having visions of turning up to the shop and having to ask Gertie to buy a copy and get me to sign it. Which she would probably have refused to do!

The day itself was taken up doing all kinds of interviews with radio stations and magazines, with me mainly trying to look and sound intelligent. After all, I was now an author, and I needed to act like one. Then we drove to the shop, which took about fifteen minutes.

'Look at all those teenage girls queueing outside,' Gertie said as we approached. 'They must be waiting for a pop star or something.'

Waterstones Piccadilly is a very big shop so I assumed the same.

'How many foking signing sessions have they got going on here tonight?' I said to Henry. 'I don't want to be sharing with a load of foking teenyboppers!'

'Just yours,' he said, smiling.

'WHAT?' said Gertie, almost spitting out a mouthful of water. 'That's completely ridiculous. Guenther's an old man. He's almost sixty.'

'I'm fifty-seven!'

In an attempt to drive home just how ridiculous Gertie thought this was, she started laughing and then looked at me pityingly, as you might look at an old dog that is about to be put to sleep.

'Erm, I'm not joking,' said Henry. 'Every person in that queue is here to meet Guenther.'

'Ha!' I said triumphantly, but in a mild state of shock. 'You're not shitting me, are you, Henry? Are these people really here to meet me?'

'They are, I promise you. They're not all girls though.'

'Most of them are,' said Gertie immediately. 'Some of them even have their mothers with them. Look, Guenther.'

She then pointed to two teenage girls in the queue who had two women standing with them.

'Foking hell, you're right.'

The thing I found strange was that our daughter Greta was about the same age at the time, and when I'd had to accompany her to an event it was usually a swimming gala or something, not a signing session by a middle-aged butcher's son from the mountains where the air is thin.

'What do you think Greta would make of all this?' I said to Gertie.

'I think she'd find it hilarious. Strange, but hilarious.'

On closer inspection, I'd say about 50 per cent of the people in the queue were female and there were just as many young fans as older, perhaps more traditional motor racing types. What's more, when they saw me get out of the car and walk towards the front door of the shop they started shouting and waving their hands in the air. I don't mind admitting that I found this slightly embarrassing at first, mainly because I had Gertie with me who was still shaking her head and saying how ridiculous it all was. But I also found it humbling. The majority of my experiences with the general public prior to this had, as I just said, been during a Grand Prix weekend, so as enthusiastic and friendly as people always were (and they have been invariably since all this started), they weren't there to see just me. These people were though, and that felt strange.

After the signing, which went very well indeed and consisted of three hundred book sales, three hundred dedications and signatures which towards the end was incredibly foking painful, and about four thousand selfies, I went back to the hotel room with Gertie.

'I still don't get why there were a lot of teenage girls there,' said Gertie.

'It must be my personality,' I said, lying back on the bed.

'Probably,' she agreed. 'Well, let's face it, it's certainly not your looks.'

2021

THE REBUILD

Boy, have I been looking forward to writing about 2021 – NOT! The only positive, I think, is that we went into the season expecting less than fok all in terms of results, and my God did it deliver. If only the same thing had happened in terms of drama and headaches. Then again, had there been no drama or headaches in my life you would be reading *Guenther Steiner's Guide to Serenity*, or something weird.

Anyway, let's give it a go and see if I can do it without bursting into tears.

One of the most challenging tasks in the lead-up to the 2021 season for me personally was having to regenerate the team as a whole and turn it into a working entity once again. In addition to us having to lay people off in Italy, during lockdown some of our staff in the UK and over in America had decided to leave for various reasons and so as well as it having been asleep for several months, the team was incomplete.

Another regeneration project I had to contend with prior to the season beginning was our relationship with suppliers. Many of these too had been mothballed in 2020 and it was hard trying to revive the relationships (or find new suppliers) while at the same time renegotiating the terms. Some of the suppliers were responsive but others weren't, and it was tough going.

What made both this and the recruitment drive easier for me was the effect it had on the team. In their eyes, the arrival of new staff and old and new suppliers coming and going at our facilities signified progress, which it did. By far the most important appointment, and the one that had the biggest effect, was our new technical director, Simone Resta. Simone had been heading up Ferrari's chassis department when we approached him. As well as spending a short stint working for my friend Fred Vasseur at Alfa Romeo, between 2014 and 2018 Simone had been Ferrari's chief designer.

Because our technical operation in Italy had also been mothballed in 2020, Simone would be resurrecting the entire department. Fortunately for us, when the budget cap came in Ferrari realized that they would have to let some people go, and when they did, we hired them. This is obviously an abridged version of what happened but you get my drift. The birth of our new technical team in Maranello signified the start of our future as they would be responsible for designing a car that would make us competitive again. At long last, the light at the end of the tunnel was visible again – just. That, more than anything, was the shot in the arm we all needed.

Before then, we still had the small matter of a pre-season test and twenty-two races across five continents to contend with. At least we had an objective though, which was to give two rookie drivers a season's worth of experience in preparation for them driving the aforementioned new car.

The biggest fight I had had on my hands prior to Simone

being hired and his team being assembled was keeping everybody motivated. Except for the drivers, of course. They were like two kids who had been locked in a foking sweet shop for a week, and the closer we got to the start of the season the more excited they became. What an opportunity though, huh? Here you go guys, race an F1 car for a season at the most iconic circuits on earth and against some of the best drivers on the planet and without any pressure or expectation. Some people would give anything for a chance like that.

In truth, although Mick and Nikita would not be judged on their results necessarily, they would most certainly be judged on their performances both on and off the track, not to mention their behaviour. If they ever needed motivating it would be for reasons other than the one I have just mentioned, and I would deal with it as and when.

With the team it was different, although only slightly. Staff retention had always been pretty good at Haas and a bond of trust existed, one that had been formed through mutual experience. Had we all been new to each other it might have been different, but by the end of 2020 we were old hands (or the majority of us were), both as colleagues and as members of the F1 community. Without wanting to sound too sentimental here, which it's fair to say I am not really known for, there was a feeling among the team going into 2021 that we could overcome pretty much anything. This, although daunting at times and not exactly inspiring, was just another test. We would get through it, just like we always did. All I had to do was keep reminding them of this, which I did. A lot.

One of the questions I am asked the most about the 2021

season is what my expectations were for Nikita Mazepin, the implication being, I think, that because he didn't do so well why on earth did I put him in the car. What, apart from the money, you mean? That was certainly a factor – obviously – but during the 2020 F2 Championship Nikita won two races, had a further four podiums and finished below only Mick, Callum Ilott, Yuki Tsunoda and Robert Shwartzman. Say what you like about the guy but that isn't bad going.

As you already know, results-wise we had no expectations at all with Nikita, but based on his track record, and the fact that he had some natural talent, my hope was that we could turn him from a competent young driver who had promise and some good results under his belt into a decent F1 driver. Did I ever think he would become world champion? Of course not. In the history of F1 there have been thirty-four champions and 776 drivers. I like a dream as much as the next idiot but ultimately I am a realist. And besides, that wasn't what I was looking for in him.

I have been trying to think of equivalents to Nikita from my rally or Jaguar days but I cannot think of any. In rallying you have something called gentlemen drivers who are basically rich guys who want to participate. They know their limitations, however, and do it only because they enjoy it. And because they can afford it, of course. Nikita was on a different level, in terms of both his age and what he could afford, which was basically anything he wanted.

What I quickly learned with Nikita was that being the son of an oligarch was as much of an obstacle to him as it was an advantage, not just from a financial point of view, but also a cultural one. Because he came from such a wealthy background he had nothing in common with anyone in the team. I'm not saying that coming from money is bad or good, it's just different. People couldn't really relate to him and vice versa. At first it wasn't a big problem but it became one later on, which I'll come on to. The cultural differences between Nikita and the team created a very similar issue, and in both instances it must have been as hard for him as it was for us. In fact, for him I'd say it might have been more difficult as at times he must have felt isolated.

Something else I quickly learned about working with Nikita (and his father, for that matter) was that it always created extreme situations. It was either enjoyable or awful, hot or cold. There was nothing in between, ever. Perhaps that is normal in Russian society but it does not make managing either a person or a team very easy and I found it unnerving sometimes. Perhaps that's the idea? A form of control. Ultimately, though, when we all arrived in Bahrain for the first and only pre-season test on 9 March 2021 it was up to him to prove to me that I had made the right decision and for him to make the most of the opportunity. After all, how many drivers who are potentially capable but are too far down the pecking order actually get an opportunity to race in Formula 1? Hardly any.

This isn't too widely known, but Mick Schumacher had already driven both a Haas and a Ferrari F1 car prior to testing in Bahrain. In 2019 he had driven for Ferrari at an in-season test and at the 2020 Abu Dhabi Grand Prix (so just three months earlier) he had sat in for Kevin at one of the practice sessions. So we decided to send Mick out first at the pre-season test in 2021 as the first session is often a journey into the unknown. Even a bit of experience, especially in this environment, can be useful.

As we feared, Mick ended up experiencing some hydraulic problems in the morning on the first day which curtailed his session, but the only other issue he reported was a sandstorm. This carried on throughout the afternoon session with Nikita but it didn't cause any problems and he managed to do a full programme. This is when I first noticed a difference between Mick and Nikita. Having already driven an F1 car and in test conditions, Mick was more considered and, dare I say it, more professional. That's not to say that Nikita was unprofessional. He wasn't. He was just a young man who was driving an F1 car for the first time having probably dreamt about it for years.

The following morning at the first session Nikita posted seventy laps which included a race simulation. Mick, who had had a frustrating first day, fared much better on day two, managing an impressive eighty-eight laps. This also included a race simulation, and the day concluded with some full-crew pit stops.

Day three went well for both drivers and we finished the test having completed almost four hundred laps. As importantly, we managed to put both drivers through a number of procedures that would stand them in good stead for the season ahead. Mick's behaviour throughout the test was exemplary. He was polite to everyone he came into contact with and always had a smile on his face. It had been the same in Abu Dhabi the year before and it complemented his behaviour on the track.

With regard to Nikita, this experience fell into the 'hot' category as his behaviour on and off the track throughout the test was very good. He was humble, attentive, fed back information well and did exactly as he was told. The only thing he did not experience during the test were any real issues which might have been met with a different response. As such, we still had no idea what to expect from Nikita in a racing environment. Or Mick, for that matter. We had all done everything we could, though, and just had to hope for the best.

THE SEASON

In a season that was packed with drama and contentious events I have been racking my ancient brain trying to think where it all began – as in, the first contentious event of 2021. Nikita deciding to film himself groping a girl in the back of a sportscar and then posting it on social media the week after being confirmed as our driver would obviously have won hands down, but that took place in 2020 so it doesn't count. No, the first contentious event I can remember from 2021 is when we launched the livery for the new car. Or should I say, the new old car.

This was contentious for two reasons: first, because the colours we used were the colours of the Russian flag and we were an American team (although to be fair they could have been the colours of the Stars and Stripes too, not to mention the Union Jack or the French tricolore – but obviously weren't); and second, because in December 2020 a two-year ban had been imposed by the Court of Arbitration for Sport relating to Russian state-sponsored doping and cover-ups at the 2014 Winter Olympics following investigations by the World Anti-Doping Agency (WADA). In February 2021 the Russian Automobile Federation confirmed that the ban would extend to Formula 1, meaning that Nikita could not race under the Russian flag. He was also prohibited from using Russian flags as well as the word 'Russia' or 'Russian' on his clothing.

Confirmation from the Russian Automobile Federation that the ban had been extended to F1 was announced around the time that we launched the livery, so despite us genuinely not being aware of the extension we were nevertheless accused by WADA of trying to circumvent the ban. In truth, the design for the livery had been agreed months earlier and we had actually done no such thing. Also, as far as we and the Mazepin family were concerned, the ban on displaying flags extended only to athletes and their clothing. And it said nothing at all about displaying just the colours of the Russian flag.

Given the ambiguity of the situation and the fact that we weren't displaying any Russian flags anywhere or the word 'Russia' or 'Russian', I was expecting WADA to let it go, but instead they threatened to take the matter to the Court of Arbitration for Sport. 'Talk to them,' the FIA suggested. 'Get a dialogue going and perhaps you can negotiate.'

When I relayed all this to Dmitry he told me that if it came to it I was to hire the best lawyers, which he would pay for, and fight it. 'I will only allow you to change the colours of the car if you have to do so by law,' he said to me, which was fair enough.

As predicted, negotiating with WADA was a slow process and by the end of 2021 they *still* had not decided whether they would take the matter to court. The decision was made for them the following year when Russia invaded Ukraine (which is obviously for another chapter), but if that hadn't happened the saga might still be ongoing.

The second contentious event I can remember at the start of

2021 took place a few minutes into Q1 at the Bahrain Grand Prix. Apart from the ongoing WADA issue everything had gone fairly smoothly since testing and while we were not expecting miracles in Bahrain (or anywhere for that matter) we were looking forward to seeing our two rookies on the grid. Also, with the Williams and the Alfas potentially being almost as rubbish as our own car, we hoped they might even have people to race against other than each other.

There is a gentlemen's agreement among F1 drivers that they will not overtake each other in the final sector of out laps during qualifying. Not only did Nikita do just that during Q1, he then made it worse by spinning off and in the process preventing Sebastian Vettel and Esteban Ocon from setting better lap times. Sebastian then received a five-place grid penalty for failing to slow down after Nikita spun off a second time, meaning that, after originally qualifying P18 in front of Mick and then Nikita, he would have to line up at the very back of the grid in P20. It is fair to say that Seb was not a happy man.

To be fair to Nikita, his first spin was down to an issue with the brake-by-wire system which made him lock up, and he had no idea about the so-called gentlemen's agreement. As with all of these experiences, it had to be treated like a learning curve.

The third contentious event of the 2021 season took place at turn three on the first lap of the race in Bahrain, so they were coming thick and fast. On coming out of the turn Nikita put the throttle on but then lost the back end and spun off into the gravel before hitting the barriers. Martin Brundle summed it up perfectly in his commentary by saying, 'As with so many things in my life he got a bit trigger happy with the throttle and went off and had his own accident.' Nikita was OK, which was the main thing, but his car wasn't, and unfortunately he had to retire. One driver down after a few hundred metres. That was good going, even for us.

For balance, Mick spun off a few corners later after the safety car had gone in, although he didn't suffer any damage. If I had to provide you with a positive from the race, apart from Mick finishing P16, it would be him eventually catching up with Latifi and experiencing what it's like to follow a car closely and have DRS. It isn't much, I know, but it's all we had.

I'm going to stop with the 'contentious events' count now as by the time we reach the end of the chapter it could be into the hundreds, and to be honest with you I do not want to know the actual score.

Race two of 2021 was the Emilia Romagna Grand Prix at Imola. The weekend got off to the worst possible start when, towards the end of FP1, Nikita crashed out causing a second red flag. The damage to the car wasn't serious, fortunately, although it cost us time in FP2.

Once again, and after having been asked not to, Nikita managed to enrage a couple of drivers during qualifying by overtaking on out laps. Antonio Giovinazzi in particular was furious as Nikita's actions prevented him from producing a flying lap. There wasn't really a lot we could say about the situation other than we would speak to him – again. He wasn't exactly endearing himself to the rest of the grid though, that's for sure. Then again, would he have given a shit about this? Probably not. It was a learning curve for me too, not just the other drivers. Once again, Nikita was saved from having to start twentieth by another unlucky driver (Yuki Tsunoda), although this time Nikita was not involved.

So, what can I tell you about the race? Not a great deal really, apart from the fact that after spinning off into the gravel Nikita clipped Latifi which sent him into the barriers and finished his race, and that Mick and Nikita finished two laps behind the winner. It was just another day at the office for Team Haas and their increasingly battle-scarred team principal.

In Portugal for race three there were yet more spins. This time, however, nothing could save Nikita from having to start right at the back of the grid with Mick just in front of him. Positives were even harder to come by at this race and the only one I can think of is that Mick finished the race a place higher than he qualified. That really is it, I'm afraid. Then again, what were we expecting?

Given the fact that I had saved his team from extinction while at the same time ensuring that he would barely have to put his hand in his pocket for a year, I was expecting a change in attitude from Gene going into the 2021 season. Furthermore, I had managed his expectations well prior to the season starting, and with brutal honesty.

'With two rookies and no development,' I said to him, 'we will be last. There are no two ways about it, Gene, so you will have to get used to the idea. It's going to be a foking tough season.'

At first Gene seemed to accept this, but after three or four races he began complaining. 'You said it was going to be tough,' he said to me, 'but I didn't realize it would be *this* tough.'

'What are you talking about, Gene? We are last, just like I said we would be. You cannot be the only team to mothball development and expect to be anything other than shit. We are where we deserve to be at the moment. Unless you can tell me any different.'

Even this blunt assessment did not seem to hit home with Gene and his remarks and extreme disappointment continued into the season. In the end I just let it go over my head and it became white noise. I don't mean to sound disrespectful by saying that, but I was practising self-preservation. The situation was bad enough without me losing my shit because of Gene's constant negativity. Regardless of who was talking, as far as I was concerned if you didn't have anything constructive to say at the time I was not interested in hearing it. No thank you.

By race four in Barcelona something had happened that, if it wasn't sorted out quickly, could make things very difficult for the team. With his performances not yet improving (and that's to say nothing of his reputation on the grid), Nikita's attitude to the people around him — the people who were trying to help him — had already started to deteriorate. The polite, responsive, helpful and sometimes even humble heir to a multi-billion-dollar fortune who we had worked so closely with at the start of the season had disappeared and in his place was somebody I had always feared was there but had hoped would remain hidden away.

Despite his father being present for some of the time and him sometimes having a couple of guys from his Formula 2 team in tow, Nikita obviously felt isolated. At the end of the day, though, they were only ever going to tell him what he wanted to hear so he was receiving no objective words of advice, except from the people he thought were against him, which was actually his team.

The balancing act for me was quite difficult as I'm sure you can imagine. Actually, that is a titanic understatement. It was a foking nightmare! On one side I had an increasingly paranoid driver who seemed to think that being rude to people was the best way of getting them to help you and whose father just happened to be the title sponsor, and on the other I had a team of people who felt intimidated and increasingly uncomfortable.

The entire situation had been exacerbated by the fact that Mick had been outperforming Nikita in almost every department from the start of the season. In fact, after nine races it was 9–0 to Mick in qualifying and 7–2 in race results. Also, instead of avoiding Mick like they were starting to do with Nikita, he remained popular with the team. As a consequence of both these factors, the relationship between Nikita and Mick also began to suffer, which helped nobody.

As a situation this wasn't too dissimilar to the one we had had with Romain at the start of 2016, except this time I would have a bit more to lose if I decided to tear the driver a new asshole (figuratively). Then again, as well as believing that Nikita was in the wrong it was also my duty to support and protect the team as best I could.

In a debrief after one of the practice sessions before the Spanish Grand Prix, during which Nikita had been rude and aggressive to his engineer and then obnoxious at the start of the debrief itself, I asked if I could speak to him afterwards. Apparently I made a comment on the pit wall during the session after Nikita had spoken rudely to his engineer that was picked up by Netflix. I said, 'That's why everyone hates you.' Unfortunately that was true at the time, which is a shame.

In our meeting after the debrief I tried to explain to Nikita that by being rude to the team all he was doing was pushing them away and making them less likely to want to work hard on his behalf. That's a pretty straightforward argument, huh? I mean, how on earth can you dispute it?

Well, Nikita was at least up for trying. In his mind even being polite to people wasn't going to help the situation, and as far as he was concerned being rude to the team and angry with everyone was perfectly acceptable. He told me that he didn't want to be loved, which I understood, but what I did not understand was his dismissal of common courtesy, not only as something that should be practised within a team as a matter of course but as something that can potentially help to get you out of a shitty situation. At the time it felt like a cultural issue, but one that was defined more by Nikita's upbringing than his nationality.

What was particularly frustrating was that slowly but surely we had started to see an improvement in Nikita's performances. Nothing seismic, but had he had the common sense to just keep his head down and work hard with the team like Mick had been doing, he not only might have become a better F1 driver, he might also have started to change people's opinions about him being in the sport. As the son of a billionaire, who despite having talent was not there on merit, Nikita had a lot to prove in that regard, but then so did Mick. The difference being that what Mick had to prove was that he was worthy of the name Schumacher.

The crux of Nikita's argument, such as it was, was something that I later christened 'Chassis-gate', and it had first come to light during the weekend of the second race at Imola. The moaning and rudeness had been happening since race one, but this took Nikita's paranoia to a completely different level, not to mention my blood pressure.

The first I knew of it was when Nikita started complaining to his race engineer that Mick was faster on the straight than he was. This quickly morphed into a claim by Nikita that Mick was driving a different car to him and that was the cause of his poor performance. We're back to the difference between reasons and excuses again, and this time there was not a reason in sight. I tried reminding Nikita and Dmitry several times that as a team we were contractually obliged to provide each of our drivers with exactly the same equipment and support, but they did not believe me. Nikita had got it into his head that Mick was at an advantage and that was the end of it.

The race in Barcelona just made matters worse, in that Mick had quite a strong race whereas Nikita did not, and by the time we got to Silverstone in July things had deteriorated further. In one final bid to try and prove that Mick was driving a different car to him, Nikita's father Dmitry paid to have a new chassis made for his son after having claimed that the chassis we had provided had been flexing which had made the car difficult to control.

Twenty years earlier chassis had indeed been prone to flexing sometimes which was down to attempts at making them as light as possible. This was finally eradicated with the introduction of side impact testing. After that, flexing became a thing of the past. I did try and explain this to Nikita and Dmitry but they did not want to know and went ahead with having a new one produced. One thing I wanted to say to Nikita and Dmitry but couldn't was that in my opinion the problems with the car were down to Nikita's lack of experience, which could have been improved upon if he had carried on working with us and altered his attitude.

Unsurprisingly the brand-new chassis brought no improvement whatsoever to Nikita's performances, which resulted in him and his father resorting to plan B, which was to threaten to pull the sponsorship. I ended up having to remind Dmitry that if he tried to do so Nikita would not have a drive, which cleared the matter up pretty quickly.

While all this was going on I stopped myself going completely mad by immersing myself whenever I could in what was happening over in Italy. As well as being new to the team, Simone Resta was new to the position of technical director, and I wanted to make sure that he was OK and that he and his team had everything they needed to try and make sure that we had a competitive car for 2022. At the end of the day, thanks to my sermons to the team about us having a bright future, the progress of Simone and his team was the lifeblood of the whole team.

I'm not sure what the catalyst was, but as the season progressed Nikita's attitude slowly began to improve and, miraculously, so did his performances. He was just like he had been during testing – polite, considered, humble and approachable – and it was good to have the original Nikita back. The results remained the same to the end of the year, which wasn't his fault, but he started having fewer accidents and managed to find some pace occasionally. Furthermore, as opposed to everybody being afraid of Nikita and avoiding him, he managed to find his place within the team.

From my own point of view, it was nice to see Nikita express some emotions other than just anger and frustration. I also got a glimpse of what being in F1 actually meant to the guy, as after making a mistake during qualifying in São Paulo, as well as being extremely apologetic to the team he almost burst into tears during an interview afterwards. I know, Guenther Steiner being nice about Nikita Mazepin? Call the foking papers! This, just like every other finely honed paragraph in what is my second piece of quality literature, has obviously been written with the benefit of hindsight, and I am far more aware these days of the challenges Nikita had to contend with coming into the sport.

As I said earlier, it is my belief that his uber-privileged background was, in some situations, as much of a hindrance to him as it was an advantage, but by the end of the 2021 season he had become a team player. He wasn't the finished article, not by any means, but he knew how to play the game and wanted to improve as much as he could and be part of the team. It took him a while to get there but you cannot ask for much more than that from a rookie.

2022

THE LIGHT AT THE END OF THE TUNNEL

I was genuinely a little bit worried before starting this section as I have already written a three-hundred-page book about the 2022 season. Having re-read that quite recently I am of the opinion that a reflective account of what happened in 2022 will actually be a lot different to the existing reactive account that was written in real time. There will also be a lot less swearing, I think. Then again, if you have read *Surviving to Drive* there could not really be more swearing. As I just said though, that was a reactive account of what was a pretty eventful and stressful season. In this book I have not been swearing nearly as much and that is because I am relaxed, calm and Zen. In fact, I am as happy as a pig in shit. Anyway, let's get on with this.

My mindset going into 2022 was the opposite to how it had been going into 2021, or even 2020. Although the pandemic had not yet taken a grip at the start of 2020, we had had a shit 2019 and the rot had already started to set in with regard to the difference in how I wanted to do things and how Gene did – as in, I wanted him to invest so that we could move forward and he did not. My mindset and mood now were far more akin to how they had been from 2016 to 2018, and that felt good. Really good.

In all honesty, as much as the progress we had been making over the past year with 2022 in mind had been by design, both literally and metaphorically, we had actually been very fortunate as assembling an entire experienced F1 design team in a matter of a few weeks would have been impossible had it not been for the budget cap forcing the Scuderia to let people go. People, incidentally, who I already knew personally and who understood not only the business model behind the Haas F1 Team but how the team worked day to day. Despite that, and despite knowing me personally, they were still willing to come and work with us, which was amazing.

I used to think that we had simply been lucky in being able to assemble such a team so quickly and had been in the right place at the right time. Then again, if the relationship had not been there in the first place it would never have happened. You make your own luck in this world and, without wanting to blow my own trumpet (although I will toot it again), it is something that I have always been pretty good at.

Morale in the team going into 2022 mirrored my own, in that it was similar to the old days. There was one issue, though, that concerned me very slightly. It does not matter how pumped or how motivated you feel, if you have spent two years coasting and being denied hope, which is basically where we had been since the start of the pandemic, you are not going to be as sharp as you need to be. Or, to use a sporting term that I have heard before many times but have no foking idea where it comes from, you're not going to be match fit.

In addition to this, we did not have to provide any reasons or excuses about why we'd been underperforming. I sometimes did to Gene but I was used to that. Although these reasons were legitimate, the fact is we became detached from having to cope with things like culpability and responsibility. Not completely, of course, but from the part that drives you to perform in a competitive environment. All I could do in an effort to counter that potential lack of edge was to make the team aware that it might exist. It would only really come back when we were starting to fight for points again.

The relationship with Uralkali and the Mazepin family continued to be OK going into 2022. In fact, if I had to describe it in one word I would probably say neutral, which given the circumstances was likely the best either of us could hope for. They too had been looking forward to us being competitive again, although at the end of the day the proof would be in the pudding and nobody would know anything until we started testing. Despite everything that had gone on between us in 2021, the Mazepins had been aware of the situation since day one and had always bought into our vision of relaunching the team as a competitive entity in 2022.

What made the situation even more trepidatious was that, as per usual, we had absolutely no idea what anyone else was doing. This always plays on your mind as a team principal, as I'm sure you can imagine, but when you're trying to paddle your team out of a river full of shit it can play on it even more. Fortunately I have always been pretty adept at decompartmentalizing 'what if' scenarios so for the sake of my own wellbeing it had to be consigned to the already overflowing 'there is fok all I can do about that' file.

In 2022 a pre-testing shakedown had been arranged at the Circuit de Barcelona-Catalunya a few days before the first test and we were the third team to go out after Red Bull and Alfa Romeo. With restrictions on aerodynamic simulations as well as testing, pre-test shakedowns had become essential for F1 teams, and I for one could not wait to get to Spain.

Nikita was the first driver in the car, and as he was coming down the straight on the first lap I noticed something strange. 'Foking hell,' I said to Ayao Komatsu. 'Look at that – he's bouncing!' Just then Nikita came on the radio: 'Sorry guys, but I genuinely cannot drive this thing. The car is literally jumping off the track.' When you see a car lifting up like that you know you have a big foking problem. I remember putting my head in my hands and thinking, what the hell have we done here? This, of course, was our first experience of the aerodynamic phenomenon known as porpoising.

I'm sure you will all have heard of porpoising, but just in case you aren't sure what it is, I will tell you in layman's terms. Porpoising is a result of ground effect and takes place when the air is sucked underneath a car in order to pull it closer to the track. What none of us realized at the time was that the faster you go, the closer the car is sucked to the track, and when it gets too close it causes the airflow to stall, meaning the downforce suddenly vanishes. At that point the car springs upwards and it all starts again. Something else we did not know at the time was that this was going to be the bane of our lives for many weeks to come and would be the cause of some big arguments. Although not all involving me, I am happy to say.

Incidentally, do you know where the word 'porpoising' comes

from? I do, but only because I read it in an article. It comes from an animal called the porpoise that lives in the sea and bobs up and down. It obviously fits as a name, but whoever thought of this must have been on foking drugs or something. I mean, really. Porpoising? Come on, guys.

Under normal circumstances you obviously would not approach another team principal to ask how they had been getting on during a test or a shakedown, and at first nobody did. I could tell that something was wrong though, and pretty soon some rumours started circulating. Every team on the grid had had to design and build a brand-new car using the ground effect philosophy and I was adamant that we could not be the only team with a bouncing car. Then again, with the luck we had been having lately, who knows?

Formula 1 is a global sport with only ten teams and is very incestuous. The things that should remain secret do (usually) but when something threatens all of us we understand that divided pain is half the pain. After speaking with some of the other team principals after the shakedown it turned out that we were certainly not the only team with a bouncing car. In fact, if the rumours were true, all ten teams were suffering from it to varying degrees. This made it easier to accept, but at the same time it had to be sorted out quickly.

'If this is the worst thing we have to deal with this season,' I said to Gertie when I called her after the shakedown, 'I will be a very happy man.'

If only.

THE INVASION

With the first day of the test taking place just two days after the shakedown the team did not have long to work on the porpoising issue. I obviously wasn't expecting us to solve it in that time but we were confident that we could make it less severe. That was my only real worry going into the test, and all in all I felt confident and quite relaxed.

When I arrived at the track on the Tuesday, so the day before the first day of the test, I was met outside the motorhome by Stuart Morrison. Normally our communications director is one of the most calm and unflappable people I know but that day he seemed agitated.

'Can I talk to you please, Guenther,' he said. 'It's urgent.'

'What the fok has happened now?' I said to him. 'OK, let's go to my office.'

As Stuart opened the door to the motorhome and went in I began to wonder what it might be. I couldn't think of anything though, which was not normal.

'Have you heard the news about Russia?' he said once the door to my office had been closed.

'No, what about it?'

'Apparently they're on the verge of invading Ukraine.'

'What? You have got to be foking joking.'

I'd had my phone on silent since arriving at the track but when I took it off it started ringing almost immediately. I also had about twenty messages and emails waiting for me. 'This is some serious shit, Stuart,' I said to him. I spent the rest of the day avoiding the press and thinking about what to do next. Not only did we have a Russian title sponsor and a Russian driver, we also had a livery in the colours of the Russian flag. While Putin rattled his sabre, the eyes of the motorsport world would be firmly fixed on us, and sooner or later we were going to have to either do or say something.

Later on that day I saw Nikita. Everybody was trying to act as normally as possible around him but the elephant in the room – the white, red and blue elephant – was getting bigger by the second. To be honest, I was a little bit worried about him at first. Whatever was happening in Russia, it was not his fault and I didn't want him to feel either isolated or uncomfortable. I ended up having a chat with him in my office, and fortunately he seemed fine. 'All I want to do is concentrate on the test,' he said, which was fine by me.

That night it took me a long time to get to sleep, and even when I did sleep I kept on waking up every few minutes. The prospect of war being declared is obviously terrible whatever the circumstances, but when you are associated with the aggressors, as in the country, it takes on a whole new meaning.

'What are you going to do?' Gertie asked when I spoke to her very early the next morning.

'That's what everyone wants to know,' I said. 'But at the moment I'm not sure.'

The first day of the test was pretty shit. Nikita had a cooling leak in the morning which curtailed his session and then Mick had issues with the floor in the afternoon which curtailed his. I was also pretty exhausted, and when I wasn't on the pit wall or hanging around the garage I spent most of my time in my office with the door closed. My phone was lighting up every few seconds but I still didn't know what to do. Half of me just wanted to remove the name of our main sponsor completely, not to mention the colours of the Russian flag. Then again, what if Russia decided not to invade? What would happen then? I couldn't win either way.

Because I was so tired I had an early night, and fortunately I slept well. Gene was now in town and staying at the same hotel and I had arranged to meet him for breakfast. As he and I sat there in the dining room the following morning the conversation flitted from the test to the situation in Russia and Ukraine. 'Everyone wants to know what we're going to do,' I said to Gene. 'But at the moment our hands are tied.'

Just then, out of the corner of my eye I saw the word NEWS-FLASH come up on one of the TV screens in the room followed by RUSSIA DECLARES WAR ON UKRAINE.

'He's done it,' I said to Gene. 'Putin's declared war.'

As shocking as this news was, it at least gave me leave to do what I had been wanting to do since finding out that this was on the cards, which was to remove Uralkali and the colours of the Russian flag from our livery and branding immediately. With the WADA situation still ongoing it was already seen as being controversial and if we did not act quickly we would get crucified by the press. In addition to this, we had already had some of our other sponsors on the phone expressing concern about being seen alongside a Russian company.

I have no idea if I was in the majority on this but despite all the threats he had been making over the past weeks I never thought for one moment that Putin would actually declare war on his neighbours. Then again, I never thought that Fernando Alonso would end up making the mother of all comebacks, so what the hell do I know?

After a quick conversation with Gene, who agreed with my plan, I went straight to the track and asked Stuart to prepare a press release while I started calling all the relevant people. First on the list after the FIA and Stefano Domenicali was Uralkali. Dmitry had been with us in Barcelona until the day before but had been called back to Moscow urgently. Now we knew why. Instead of calling him I decided to call the chairman of Uralkali, who was based in America and who I had a pretty good relationship with. Initially he asked me to hang on for a few days but I refused. By procrastinating we were in danger of being adversely linked to one of the most serious geopolitical situations since World War Two and I could not allow that to happen. While the chairman was obviously disappointed he understood my reasoning, so that was that. I had a feeling it wouldn't end there, however, as he still had to break the news to Dmitry and the other board members. Anyway, at least the call had been made.

Before sending out the press release, Gene arranged a board meeting with Haas Automation just to get everything cleared. Because the majority of the board members were based in California we had to wait a few hours until they were awake and had had their first kombucha of the day. Whereas the majority agreed with what I was proposing, one or two of them, just like the chairman of Uralkali, wanted us to wait and see if the situation changed. 'We cannot do that,' I said to them. 'For a start we would lose every other sponsor we have, but in addition to that our reputation would be destroyed. That press release needs to go out now.'

Fortunately, instead of labouring their point the board members saw sense, and on the afternoon of 24 February, Stuart Morrison sent out the following statement:

> Haas F1 Team will present its VF-22 in a plain white livery, minus Uralkali branding, for the third and final day of track running at Circuit de Barcelona-Catalunya on Friday, 25 February. Nikita Mazepin will drive as planned in the morning session with Mick Schumacher taking over in the afternoon. No further comment will be made at this time regarding team partner agreements.

With regard to the press and the public on social media this had the desired effect, and we went from being on the cusp of becoming a global sporting pariah to being a team that had a conscience and that had acted quickly and appropriately.

The only other person I spoke to personally that day was Nikita. He had been fine the day before and when I spoke to him he told me that despite things having changed he was still focused on the test and on his career as an F1 driver. At the time the FIA were in the process of making a decision about how the invasion might affect both the Russian Grand Prix and Russian drivers but I did not mention that to him. At this juncture there was no point.

The test, incidentally, went much better on day two and we finally started to see some of the potential that had basically been our lifeblood for as long as I could remember. Had that not materialized, I'm not sure what I would have done, to be honest with you. The Uralkali situation had been yet another thorn in the side of my strong but beleaguered team and only good news from the garage was going to improve the mood and give us the strength we needed to keep going. That all sounds a bit dramatic, I suppose, but it's exactly how it was. Nobody goes into F1 for the good of their health. In fact, it usually has a detrimental effect in that regard. You do it because you want to compete. We were almost there.

When I arrived back at the hotel that night I made the stupid mistake of taking my phone off silent. No sooner had the threat of us being excommunicated by the sporting world disappeared than a rumour that we were about to go under had started circulating. People had obviously assumed that we had terminated our agreement with Uralkali, which we had not, and so had lost their investment. Either way, after having had some assurances from certain people about what might happen if we did have to terminate our agreement with the company I wasn't too worried. I was exhausted and felt like I had aged five years in two days, but not worried.

Believe it or not, the following day, which was the final day of the test, was actually more stressful than the previous two put together. I'm being serious. By the time I got to the track the mechanics had found an oil leak in the car, and to cut what turned out to be an increasingly depressing story short, we ended up managing just nine laps all day which was about 180 short of what we were hoping for. In real terms this meant we had had just one full day of testing out of a possible three, not to mention everything else we'd had to contend with. It was far from ideal but we just had to keep our heads down and hope that our luck would start to change.

THE REPLACEMENT

Arriving home and seeing my family after I have been away is always a pleasure, but when I walked through the door after the test in Barcelona I could almost have cried with joy. The situation with Uralkali and Nikita was far from over, I knew that, but in order to be able to cope with the next stage (whatever that was) I needed to recharge my batteries and spend some time with the people closest to me.

In total, I think I had four or five days of peace and quiet before things started to ramp up again. There were plenty of emails and messages in that time but most of them were just speculation from friends and colleagues about what the FIA might decide to do about the Russian Grand Prix and about Russian drivers. In truth, I think everybody already knew that the Russian Grand Prix would have to go, which just left the drivers. Or, as far as F1 was concerned, *the* driver.

Speaking of drivers, the speculation that was circulating about Russian drivers potentially being banned from racing in certain countries opened up the floodgates to drivers who would have liked to take their place. I cannot remember how many contacted me in total – six or seven, maybe – but their messages varied from a subtle 'Hey Guenther, how are you? Just in case you need a driver in the coming weeks I am available' to a slightly blunter 'Guenther, when you get rid of the spinning Russian, call me!'

By 2 March, not only had the Russian Grand Prix been axed from the 2022 calendar but a number of countries around the world had issued sanctions against Russian nationals that would prevent Nikita from being able to race there. Because of the WADA situation he wasn't actually racing under a Russian flag at the time but the chances were that, rightly or wrongly, he still would not have been welcome. If we decided to stick with Nikita, not only would we be antagonizing these countries but we would also be intrinsically linked to the aggressors in this new war. As I have already said, I could not allow that to happen.

'We have to sever ties with both Uralkali and Nikita immediately,' I said to Gene. 'It's the only way forward for us. Anything less will make us complicit in Putin's war.'

Had Gene disagreed with me I would have walked there and then, but fortunately he didn't. 'OK, set the wheels in motion at your end,' he said, 'and I'll deal with the board.'

After having stayed up for most of the night arranging things with Stuart who was over in the UK, on Saturday 5 March we released what would hopefully be our final statement about our Russian affiliations, at least for some time:

> Haas F1 Team has elected to terminate, with immediate effect, the title partnership of Uralkali, and the driver contract of Nikita Mazepin. As with the rest of the Formula One community, the team is shocked and saddened by the

invasion of Ukraine and wishes for a swift and peaceful end to the conflict.

As you might well be aware, the fallout from this with regard to both Nikita and Uralkali went on for quite a while, and due to the legal situation I had better keep my mouth shut. Suffice to say that neither was particularly happy with our decision to sever ties, but we knew that would be the case. In order to make an omelette you have to break some eggs, and to us this would give us a clean slate. The lawyers could clean up the mess, and would.

Before the press release went out I had already started looking for a replacement for Nikita. In fact, that process had started shortly after Gene and I had made the decision to cancel his contract. The initial list I drew up of drivers I thought would be suitable was quite short, and while discussing it with Gene he had an idea.

'Have you contacted Magnussen?' he said.

'Fok, Kevin! Of course!' To be honest, I hadn't even thought about our little Danish friend but it was a great idea. Not only did he know the team inside out, he was also an experienced driver. If I could get him, he'd be perfect. 'Let me call him now,' I said to Gene.

Since leaving Haas, Kevin had spent a year racing for Chip Ganassi in the IMSA Sportscar Championship and had recently signed a contract with Peugeot to drive in the World Endurance Championship alongside Jean-Éric Vergne and Paul di Resta. Although I hoped he might be interested I had no idea how tight his contract with Peugeot might be or whether he would even want to speak to the man who had brought his F1 career to a premature end.

The initial conversation, which took place less than half an hour after I had spoken to Gene, lasted less than five minutes. First of all I asked Kevin if he was interested, which he said he was, and then I asked him what the situation was with Peugeot. 'I think they'll be OK,' he said. 'Sebring isn't for another week so they can find a replacement.'

'OK,' I said to him. 'Let's try and do it.'

Both Kevin and I got to work immediately on trying to bring him back into the team and after a few days we were almost there. Peugeot were very helpful and said that as long as they could find a replacement in time for 24 Hours of Sebring, which was the first race of the WEC season, they would be happy to release him. We obviously had to pay them compensation, which was fair enough, but all in all they were very good to deal with and very fair. In the end a compatriot of Kevin's called Mikkel Jensen took his place in the WEC, and on 9 March we put out yet another foking press release. This time, however, instead of letting the world know that we had severed ties with a driver, we were letting it know that we were bringing one back.

This was one of those situations that just felt right, which is why it was all done and dusted in a matter of a few days. Normally when making such an important appointment you would take your time, but we didn't have much of that. In fact, the second test in Bahrain was due to start just twenty-four hours after the press release went out. Everything was in hand though. Kevin had signed his contract and was on his way to Bahrain, the

THE REPLACEMENT / 249

team were excited about seeing him and I still hadn't had a heart attack or even a nervous breakdown. Then again, the season had not even started yet and we had a test and twenty-two races ahead of us. I had no idea what was going to happen, of course, but at this point in time nothing would have surprised me.

THE VIKING COMEBACK

The test in Bahrain was delayed for us because of a freight issue (of course it was!) and after a lot of toing and froing we were eventually granted some extra testing time to compensate. Because of how things had gone so far this year I was almost expecting drama to materialize and would probably have missed it if it had not appeared. It certainly made life interesting.

Our reserve driver Pietro Fittipaldi went out on the first day of the test and he had a pretty good run. He had obviously been disappointed at not getting Nikita's drive but for the sake of us realizing the potential of the new car we could not turn down the opportunity of replacing a rookie with an experienced driver. Eventually he understood that, and by the time he arrived in Bahrain he was his usual happy self again.

Mick had the first run on day two of the test and, thanks to an oil leak, he had a difficult morning, managing just twenty-three laps. In the afternoon it was Kevin's turn. This, as you can imagine, received an awful lot of attention. It had been sixteen months since he had even sat in an F1 car and people had been asking whether he would be able to cope. 'He's already had six full seasons in F1 prior to this,' I said to a journalist. 'Of course he will cope. Although his neck might be a bit foked up by the end of it.'

Kevin ended up banking sixty laps during his session *and* the fastest lap of the day.

'How was that?' I asked him after the session.

'It took me a couple of laps to get the hang of it again,' he said, 'but yeah, it was great. Although I think my neck's broken.'

Fortunately he was only kidding about his neck being broken, although he said it was pretty sore.

The final day of the test went pretty much like the second day in terms of laps and data, and if I had to summarize how things had gone generally I would say that we had a pretty fast car on our hands but with one or two reliability issues. Fortunately, unlike the porpoising saga which was ongoing (but improving for us, thank God), these were all fairly minor and we were confident that by the time we turned up in Bahrain again for the first race of the season the following week they would all be sorted out.

After three encouraging practice sessions in Bahrain on Friday and Saturday morning (encouraging, as in, there were no major issues to speak of) we lined up for Q1 with smiles on our faces and some very welcome hope in our hearts. I appreciate that I might be in danger of sounding like a stuck record with regard to how long the road out of Shitsville had been but you will have to cut me some slack. There were never any guarantees that we would have a fast car with some potential, and all things considered – a brand-new design team, etc. – it could easily have gone the other way. It wasn't just hope we were experiencing then (as well as excitement), it was relief.

Thinking back, my hopes for qualifying at Bahrain prior to Saturday were to get both cars through to Q2. At the time I could not even bring myself to think past that and would have been very happy if it had happened. Then, when Kevin got P5 in Q1 and Mick P13 my ambition started to expand a little. In Q2 Mick finished P12, which was his best qualifying performance to date. Kevin then got P6, which guaranteed Haas our first top-ten appearance on the grid since Brazil in 2019. Could things get any better? Actually, they could.

During Q2 a hydraulic issue had started to give Kevin some problems and he could not go out in Q3 until it had been sorted out. As the minutes ticked by I started getting used to the fact that we might not get out at all. Then, with just over three minutes of the session left, I got word that the problem had been fixed.

By the time he left the pit lane there were just two minutes and fifty seconds left on the clock – he had just one lap. Ayao Komatsu, who was next to me on the pit wall, started getting animated but I could not look. You already know that I am not normally a nervous person but the surprise of getting this far was having an effect on me. After Kevin had been out for about a minute I could not look away any longer, for if the final third of his lap was anything to go by he was fast. 'That's P7,' said Kevin's engineer after he crossed the line. 'Welcome back, mate.' Now I was the one getting animated. Jeezoz, I was so foking happy!

As much as we wanted to celebrate after qualifying we had to hold back our emotions as only half the job had been done. We were there to compete and score points and were on the verge of being able to do just that for the first time in twenty-eight races. Twenty-eight! That feeling of expectation was one of the emotions

I had missed the most since everything had gone to shit and I wanted it to stay for as long as possible.

The only thing that concerned me now was whether Kevin would be race ready. Getting used again to driving an F1 car in a testing or even a qualifying environment was completely different, and having been out for over a year I did wonder how he would cope. What cheered me up slightly was the knowledge that Kevin is without fear and is a born fighter. He's also super fit, and I knew for sure that he would be relishing a situation like this. Also, none of the other drivers on the grid had raced in one of the new cars before. He'd be fine.

Kevin got off to a very good start, and before the end of lap one he had moved up to P5. Unfortunately he was not able to hold the position and moved back to P7, but he was driving really well.

'He seems confident,' I said to Ayao.

'He does,' he replied. 'He's looking good.'

By lap forty-seven Kevin had pitted three times but was still P7. Then, after losing his position to Pierre Gasly who was in P8 before taking it back again, we informed Kevin that the Frenchman had then had to retire, resulting in a safety car. Gasly's retirement was actually quite dramatic as after pulling over, the rear of his car just exploded. He set what must have been a new world record for somebody removing themselves from an F1 car. God, he was quick. It must have been seriously scary though.

The safety car went in on lap fifty, by which time I had become resigned to the prospect of us only scoring six miserable points. Six! What a complete foking disaster (I like my sarcasm blunt, you know). Then, three laps before the end of the race, Max Verstappen started slowing down and ended up crawling into the pits.

'Look at the gap between Kevin and Bottas,' I said to Ayao. 'Twelve seconds! That's eight points in the bag.'

'Don't say that!' he snapped. 'This is Haas, remember. Anything can happen and probably will.'

Ayao was right. If Kevin had been abducted by aliens on the final lap and then been replaced with the ghost of Niki Lauda, nobody would have batted an eyelid.

On lap fifty-six, the penultimate lap of the race, Sergio Pérez's car went the same way as Verstappen's and we were now on the cusp of winning ten points.

'What's the gap between Kevin and Bottas?'

'You can see what the gap is!' said Ayao. 'Look on the fucking screen!'

With the Finn roughly sixteen seconds behind the Dane I knew it was impossible for Valtteri to catch Kevin, even with our luck. I just wanted confirmation.

With no flying saucers or ghosts of dearly departed grumpy Austrian F1 drivers in the vicinity, Kevin came over the line in P5. My immediate response to this, apart from smiling and hugging lots of different people, was to congratulate my new driver. 'Kevin, that was some foking Viking comeback!' I said over the radio. 'Foking great. I cannot believe it.' It was and always will be one of the most special moments in my professional life. In fact, Kevin summed the situation up perfectly. 'All the hard work and all the shitty results over the last three years,' he said in reply to me, 'have finally paid off.' I couldn't have put it better myself. 'Kevin, this is foking medicine,' I said to him later on. 'I needed this.'

Achieving something from a platform of adversity will always be much sweeter than achieving it from an advantage or even a standing start. It is the ultimate test in any sport, and when you succeed it delivers the ultimate high and the ultimate motivation. It's addictive. We all wanted more.

THE DILEMMA

I haven't really talked about Mick very much so far so allow me to bring you up to speed. I think I have already stated that Mick's behaviour had been good from day one, and by the time we left Bahrain in 2022 my opinion had not changed very much. He had had the best result of his career so far at the race, finishing P11, and was excited about the season ahead. With an experienced driver like Kevin on the other side of the garage, not to mention the new car, he had an excellent opportunity to move forward and consolidate his own place in the team. The ball was in his court, and at the very start of the season I would have put money on him hitting it back over the net.

The Bahrain Grand Prix was the first race of a double-header with Saudi Arabia, and we arrived there to the news that some Houthi rebels had started attacking an oil refinery about 10 miles from the track. Given what I said earlier about us attracting drama, I did not even flinch when I found out about it, although as you would expect the future of the Grand Prix was immediately thrown into doubt. Surprise missile attacks by dissident Shia Islamist military organizations tend to have that effect, so I am told.

The drama continued when, after having been given the go-ahead from the Saudi government to continue with the race weekend, Kevin had to retire due to mechanical failure at the start of FP2 without clocking a single lap.

This was nothing, though, compared to what happened during qualifying. Both drivers got through to Q2 which was the perfect start but then at turn twelve during a flying lap Mick lost control and went straight into the barrier. Due to the speed he was travelling at, the first thing that came to mind when I saw it happen was Romain's crash at Bahrain, except this time there were no flames and the car did not split in two. It was still a huge crash and there was a delay in Mick responding to his engineer. As with Romain's escape, this felt like an age. He was evidently dazed when he came over the radio but said he was OK. After being taken to the trackside medical centre he was then transferred to a nearby hospital, but only as a precautionary measure.

Once we'd learned that Mick was going to be OK we then had to deal with the fallout of the crash. I suppose I might get criticized for putting it into monetary terms, but as the person who was responsible for the budget, I had no choice. 'Roughly between half a million and a million,' was the news I gave to Gene. I then had to make a decision regarding the race. Either I asked the guys to work through the night to build a new car so that if he was well enough Mick could start the race from the pit lane, or we just ran with one car instead.

In the end it didn't take me long to decide. This was race two of a double-header and if you included the second test, the guys in the garage had been either working or travelling for three long weeks. It would not have been fair to put them under so much pressure, especially with Mick having to start from the pit lane. We were now back in the business of scoring points again and the chances of him doing so from that position would have been slim at best.

After making it through to Q3 Kevin managed P10 in qualifying and his reward for putting in another solid performance was two points after finishing the race P9. Leaving Saudi Arabia with twelve points in the can was tremendous and the only downside was that we also had a repair bill of close to a million dollars.

By the time we arrived in Monaco for round seven Mick hadn't had any more accidents. But at the same time he still had not scored any points. That too was starting to become a worry for me. After all, the potential was there – everyone was agreed on that – and it was up to the drivers, at least primarily, to turn that potential into points. Mick was certainly feeling the pressure by this point, but then he needed to. He was no longer a rookie and this was not Formula 2. It was Formula 1, which is supposed to be home to the twenty best drivers in the world. Pressure or not, he needed to start driving like one of them – quickly.

If you had to equate the Haas F1 Team in my era with a Grand Prix circuit it would have to be Spa or Monaco, for the very simple reason that you never know what's going to happen at those places. Although I am writing this with a smile on my face (it's amazing what some therapy and a truckload of foking tranquilizers can do), at the time the joke about Haas being unpredictable was starting to wear thin, at least with me. Apart from Max Verstappen winning at least 90 per cent of the races these days, nobody knows what is going to happen when you turn up for a race weekend. Even so, once you're on the road to progress and are performing reliably on and off the track you can start making predictions. This is where I had hoped we would be at this point in the season, but we weren't. In fact, a few more results like the two just past, which gave us nothing above P14, and we would be in danger of becoming predictably bad.

Qualifying at Monaco was a mixed bag (Kevin P13 and Mick P15) but the poor show was down to luck as much as anything, or should I say a lack of it. This continued into the race when Kevin had to retire due to an issue with the power unit. Oh well, I remember saying to myself, at least it cannot get any worse. Step forward Mr Mick Schumacher.

After being involved in an accident early on and coming in for a new front wing, Mick went back out, and a lap or two later he lost control at Piscine corner and went straight into the barriers. This time his car split completely in two which again put me in mind of Romain. Fortunately there was no fireball to go with it and after a few seconds he had confirmed to his engineer that he was OK.

I have tried very hard indeed not to repeat what I wrote in *Surviving to Drive*, but the point that came to mind as soon as I knew that Mick was OK, which I am pretty sure is what I wrote in that book, is that when a driver writes a car off once during a season because of human error you forget about it. It's just one of those things, and if you let it get to you, you're an idiot. When a driver writes off two cars in seven races during a twenty-two race season, you start asking questions. Gene was going to go ballistic – I knew that – and he had every right to. What could I say though? He was expecting me to call him and say that we had scored points and I had to tell him that we had scored no points and would have to spend another fortune.

By now it had become clear to me that Kevin's presence in the team was actually having a detrimental effect on Mick. All things considered Mick had had a pretty good season in 2021, but when Kevin arrived he'd gone from being the fastest driver in the team to the second fastest. As opposed to accepting this and trying to improve, Mick had started taking risks. Risks that were affecting his state of mind, his performances and the team's budget. Something had to change.

THE TURNAROUND

In Canada we got a reminder that the porpoising issue had not gone away, not by any means. By the time we arrived there for round eight, Mercedes had just four podium finishes to their name (three for George Russell and one for Lewis Hamilton), whereas the season before at this point they had had three wins and seven podiums, and the season before that seven wins and thirteen podiums. With almost every other team including us having seen an improvement in the porpoising issue since the start of the season, and with Toto Wolff most definitely not being where he wanted to be in either of the championships, he was seriously pissed, and during a team principals' meeting at the circuit on the Friday before the race the whole thing came to a head.

At some point during the meeting porpoising came up and pretty quickly the conversation became heated. After having been told off by Stefano Domenicali at the start of the meeting for talking, I was saying nothing, and while complaining about how the whole porpoising thing had been handled and about the fact that every other team seemed to have made progress with it except for Mercedes, all of a sudden Toto hit the foking roof, just like his cars had been doing. I'm paraphrasing here, but addressing the other team principals he said something along the lines of, if one of his cars went into the wall because it was bottoming out or too stiff he would come looking for us. Really? He wouldn't have to look very far. *I'm at the end of the foking paddock, Toto, as per usual!*

It's the only time I have ever seen or heard Toto say something even remotely irrational. Not being able to compete for wins and titles was something he was not used to, and the shift in expectation from winning races and securing podium finishes to bouncing up and down and finishing eighth was obviously to blame.

I and one or two other team principals said after that meeting that because Netflix were there he might have been doing it for the cameras, but on reflection that isn't Toto's style. He has always been quite sceptical about the whole Netflix thing and sees it purely as a bit of entertainment. Then again, that didn't mean he was suddenly going to put on shoulder pads and turn into Joan foking Collins. His pain, passion and frustration were real that day, and to be honest, it was good to see. Not because I wanted to watch him suffer. I did not. I just wanted him to know what it was like to be a bit shit.

At the time, some people claimed that Toto lost his temper because he is entitled and because things had stopped going his way. That, let me tell you, is complete bullshit. Contrary to popular belief, Toto Wolff does not come from a privileged background, and whatever you might think of him he has got where he is today through a mixture of hard work, application, talent and endeavour. So what if he looks like a cross between Spock from *Star Trek* and Frank Grillo? I like him.

From our own point of view Canada was a potential turning

point as instead of qualifying being a mixed bag, which had usually been the case, both drivers made it to Q3 and ended up blocking out the third row of the grid, Kevin in P5 and Mick P6. Although he hadn't come away with anything, Mick's performances had been improving and he seemed to be talking to Kevin a lot more. If anyone needed a mentor, Mick did, and I was hoping it would play out that way.

It was about this time that my well-known war of words with Mick's uncle Ralf started. You remember that? It got more headlines than some of the foking races back then. He and I have since buried the hatchet (stop press: we've fallen out again!), but I don't mind admitting that the timing of Ralf's outbursts could not have been worse. It made what had started to become a difficult relationship worse and helped to drive a wedge between myself and Mick. With hindsight, as the principal of the team I should have risen above this, but I did not. That is one of many things I would change if I had my time again, as well as kicking Ralf's ass down the paddock instead of just thinking about it! In 2022 I wanted his blood.

That last paragraph provided a nice break between some good news about qualifying and the inevitable shit news about the race. Yes, you guessed it, despite us blocking out the third row of the grid in what was our best qualifying performance ever, we did not manage to convert this success into a single foking point. Kevin was the driver at fault this time when he decided to take on Hamilton (and lost his front wing in the process), and if Mick had not suffered engine failure he would have ended up well inside the points. That and the qualifying result prevented me from committing hara-kiri after the race and I was sure that it was just a matter of time before Mick started scoring. He knew that too, which was far more important, and remained in good spirits.

I remember the build-up to Silverstone, which was the next race, for two reasons, neither of which is a good memory. The first one is an interview I saw with Bernie on the Friday before the race in which he said he would take a bullet for President Putin. Even if that were the case, why the hell would you say something like that? Tens of thousands of people had already died because of that man's stupid foking war so the comment was in very bad taste. I was actually quite angry with him.

The second reason I remember the build-up to Silverstone is because I was starting to feel the pressure a little bit. Things like that don't usually bother me but the fact that we had only managed to score two points from the last seven races had been playing on my mind. It had also been playing on the minds of the press, and with good reason. After all, they were only asking the same questions I had been asking myself, as in, what the hell had gone wrong?

Qualifying at Silverstone was a disaster (Kevin P17 and Mick P19) but the race itself was amazing. For once we got everything right – the pace, the strategy and the performances (from everybody) – and we ended up scoring double points. Kevin finished P10 scoring one point and Mick P8 scoring four. Mick drove his heart out that day and I was very, very pleased for him. Actually, if you ever get a chance to listen to it (it will probably be on YouTube), Mick's reaction over the radio immediately after the race is excellent. You can hear the relief in his voice, and after thanking the team over and over again he says a few swear words and then apologizes! Swearing over the team radio is obligatory in F1 these days, just ask Yuki Tsunoda.

The next race, which was the sprint in Austria, brought up the issue of team orders, which Mick had never had to deal with before. Both drivers made it through to Q3 with Kevin in P6 and Mick P7. The danger was, of course, that they might race each other from the start so I sat them down before the race and informed them that, if it became an issue, *we* — as in the team — would be the ones who would decide who was faster.

In the end we did not need to apply team orders until towards the very end of the race. The decision itself was a contentious one, although it resulted in points. Mick was following Kevin and was probably the faster of the two at the time. The problem was that Mick was being followed by Hamilton, who was faster than both of them. To cut a long story short, instead of allowing Mick to try and pass Kevin, which might have resulted in Hamilton passing both, we ordered him to stay exactly where he was for as long as possible, which he did. As a consequence, Hamilton passed Mick with a couple of laps to go, scoring the last available point, but he could not catch Kevin, who scored two points, which was all thanks to Mick.

At the time Mick was bitterly disappointed but after the race I sat him down and explained exactly why we had done it. He understood because he's sensible, unlike some members of his fanbase. Jeezoz Christ, they foking hated me after that! I used to love being told by people what had been written about me on social media. I was their public enemy number one, two, three, four and five. Sorry, Mick fans, I was just doing my job!

THE POLE

The next six races produced jack shit in terms of points which took us back to square one. This time it was a mixture of bad luck, bad performances and bad decisions, both on our part and on the part of the FIA. Since the start of the season there had been probably a dozen or so instances which had resulted in us losing either places or points.

The FIA issue finally came to a head at a meeting later on in the season in which they admitted that mistakes had been made which had led to an uneven distribution of black and orange flags. Nice admission, but that did not get us the points or places back. It was infuriating at the time, and to be honest with you it still is a little bit. I could handle the mistakes that we made as a team and always did everything in my power to rectify them. What I could not handle and what I could not do anything about were the mistakes made by the governing body – continual mistakes, I should say – that ended up costing us points. That, my friends, should not happen in any sport, ever.

The final five races of 2022 were punctuated by two events that kind of summed up not just our season but our seven years on the grid. The first one took place at Suzuka during FP1. Mick was on an in-lap and somehow managed to crash, causing $700,000 of damage. On an in-lap. Really? His excuse was that it was wet at the time, but no other drivers went off. It isn't just the budget that is affected when something like this happens. For a start, team morale takes a hammering, not to mention your reputation. We were trying to bring in a new title sponsor at the time and things like that do not help at all.

The second event is one that I am far happier to recall. It took place at Interlagos during the penultimate weekend of the season and is probably the team's most celebrated achievement to date. I am, of course, referring to the pole position that we got for the sprint race.

The biggest leveller (apart from money) that you can have in F1 is wet weather. I think I said in my first book that it results in the rich bastards at the top who have all the expectation shitting their shorts and the poor teams at the bottom rubbing their hands. In Q1 of the sprint race in Brazil the weather worked both for and against us with Mick going out in Q1 and Kevin going through to Q2. From memory, Mick had decided to stay on intermediaries whereas Kevin had changed to softs and because the track had started to dry out Kevin was about three seconds faster.

The weather in Q2 remained changeable but again after switching to softs Kevin posted a good lap and got through to Q3. By this time the sky was black and the heavens were in danger of opening so we decided to put Kevin on softs with enough fuel for just one lap. What worked in our favour was that we were situated closest to the exit of the pit lane and when the cars started queueing up for the start of the session we were at the front.

When the lights finally turned to green Kevin went out and

immediately posted a lap time of 1:11.674. It was quick, but we needed the heavens to open – fast! As I was sitting there on the pit wall next to Ayao Komatsu and Pete Crolla drops of rain suddenly started falling on the pit lane.

'Where does the lap put me?' Kevin asked Mark, his engineer.

'You're P1, mate,' he replied.

The rain was now starting to fall heavily and the other drivers were about to begin their second laps. Pérez then went quick in the first sector but when Russell went off at turn four the session was red-flagged.

'How long is it going to rain for?' I asked Pete.

'At least half an hour,' he told me.

With just eight minutes of the session left, that was it – we were on pole!

The celebrations that followed this have been well documented and although I did not manage to see this in person they began with Kevin jumping up and down on his car and saying things like 'Foking yes!' a lot. My own most vivid memory of that day is walking from the pit wall to the garage and hearing the crowd go crazy. You cannot put a price on moments like that and it is one that I will remember and treasure for the rest of my life.

But forget about me and Kevin for a moment. The people who deserved this more than anybody were the team. Not just the team at Interlagos but the team at Banbury, Maranello and in North Carolina. All of them. This was their Championship, and having been involved in getting together nearly all of them made me feel very proud. During the sprint race normality quickly took hold and we finished P8 with a point. It was our final point of the season but it was without doubt the sweetest.

THE POLE

On the Monday after the main race, in which we somewhat predictably bagged P14 and a DNF, Gene and I made the difficult decision not to retain Mick's services for 2023. I'd been talking to Nico Hülkenberg for some time and the prospect of us having two experienced drivers in place for the first time since 2020 was too much to resist.

As I predicted, Mick's reaction when I told him was one of disappointment but he said he understood, just like he had when I told him why we had had to implement team orders. Like so many things, my relationship with Mick had been misrepresented by the press and the media almost from day one, which had done him no favours whatsoever. I was OK. I was already an old man, and if Gene ever decided to get rid of me (surely he would not dare!) I knew I'd be OK. Mick, on the other hand, was at the very start of his career, and in my opinion his career had been continuously damaged for the sake of a few headlines.

If I had my time with Mick again I would encourage him to employ a manager and/or an adviser. Somebody who has experience in racing and who can mentor him. You cannot go into a major sport with the amount of responsibility and pressure he had on his shoulders without having someone like that in your entourage. It's ridiculous. His father, Michael, had become world champion at the age of twenty-two and had had Willi Weber by his side for years. Why didn't Mick have someone like that?

Look, Mick Schumacher has plenty of talent – that is not up for debate – but in my opinion that talent has not been nurtured correctly. I thought I was doing my bit by giving him the chance to cut his teeth in an F1 car but in the end it wasn't enough. Everyone should have done more, including him.

PIT STOP

RIVALRIES

Although I have always been aware of, and in some cases have been fascinated by, rivalries in motorsport, I never considered the anatomy of such things until I started working in the industry. The very first thing I learned was that if you aren't in any way competitive either as a team or an individual you won't have any rivals because nobody cares. It's as simple as that. They only begin to form once you start taking something away from somebody else. A little bit of success, in other words. Also, there are no rules with regard to how long a rivalry might last or even how it might manifest itself. And it won't always be a Prost versus Senna situation. A rivalry is a state of mind, basically. At least from within. A state of mind that will affect different people in different ways, depending on who has got the upper hand. If they gather momentum, they will often start filtering down to fans, friends, family, the media, and anyone else who is interested. That's when things start becoming exciting and when prolonged and well-documented rivalries such as Prost versus Senna and Hunt versus Lauda attain legendary status.

In my two years at the Jaguar Racing F1 Team, where I worked under the great Niki Lauda, I didn't experience one sniff of rivalry, and for the very simple reason that we were shit. You think I had some bad years with Haas? Trust me, they were nothing compared to those two years. Partly due to a load of internal rivalries, which I suppose is kind of ironic, plus a whole host of other reasons that I could probably fill an entire book with, Jaguar were on a different level to Haas. What made it worse was that the expectation was high when Niki and I joined the team and we were supposed to be competing for the Championship within three years. The team was owned by Ford who, despite their big ideas and good intentions, didn't have the commitment or the money to make it work. They also didn't have the experience needed and seemed to think that bringing Niki Lauda in would be like waving a magic wand. It wasn't, and at the end of their fourth season on the grid, Jaguar were bought out by Red Bull, who have obviously fared a little bit better.

The first time Haas started turning heads on the grid was in 2018 when we finished fifth in the Constructors' Championship. We were a small team that was overperforming, and although nothing major really happened in terms of external rivalries, the other teams started taking much more of an interest in us. One thing we did have at the team during that period was an internal rivalry between Kevin Magnussen and Romain Grosjean. Romain had been with us right from the start and when Kevin joined in 2017 they didn't see eye to eye.

In terms of ability and success they were pretty much level pegging, but they also both had a reputation for being fiery and unpredictable, on the track and off it. Perhaps predictably then (especially as they were driving for us), instead of that rivalry manifesting itself in a respectful but hard-fought battle for points like it should have, they started taking stupid risks. I told them that what they were doing was stupid but I knew just by looking at them that they weren't listening to me. The rivalry had become an unhealthy obsession for both drivers and it was threatening to turn toxic.

I mentioned this briefly earlier, but it finally came to a head at Silverstone in 2019 when, at turn three on the first lap, they made contact and put each other out of the race. This was inexcusable, and as they limped back to the garage I got on the radio and told them – very calmly, which was surprising given how foking angry I was – that as soon as they got back I wanted to talk to them both in my office. The discussion that followed between the three of us was of course the one that gained a certain amount of notoriety as Netflix had a microphone in my office (although not a camera) and recorded the whole thing, which was later included in an episode of *Drive to Survive*.

I finished off the meeting by saying that if they weren't prepared to alter their behaviour and start working for the team I did not want them and they could fok off somewhere else. I cannot think of a time in my career when I have been so foking pissed. Instead of apologizing, though, and promising not to do it again, which I think would have been advisable, Kevin climbed out of his chair and stormed out of the office and in doing so smashed my office door. In the short term this was all forgotten about very quickly as despite the histrionics both he and Romain did alter their behaviour and stopped behaving like assholes. The following spring, however, it started to make a comeback.

I can't remember where I was exactly but shortly after the next series of *Drive to Survive* had started I was getting into my car when somebody shouted something like, 'Hey Guenther, do not fok smash my door!' At first I thought he must have been an escaped lunatic or something and I just ignored him. Then, later on that day, it happened a second time. 'Do not fok smash my door, Guenther!' Once again I ignored them.

Over the next two or three days I must have had at least two or three hundred people shout something like 'Do not fok smash my door!' It was time to call Stuart Morrison.

'What the foking hell's going on, Stuart?' I said to him. 'People keep shouting at me in the street not to fok smash their door.'

'Ah, it's started then.'

'What has started? What the fok are you talking about?'

'The new series of *Drive to Survive*.'

'Yes, so what? You know I don't watch it.'

'You remember your meeting last season after Silverstone with Kevin and Romain. The one where Kevin—'

He didn't need to finish the sentence. I did it for him. 'Smashed my foking door! Now I get it. You mean, they recorded the meeting and used it for the show?'

'Yes,' said Stuart. 'I told you they had.'

'Did you? Oh shit, I can't have been listening. Well, at least it explains why people are shouting it at me every five minutes. They get excited by some strange shit these people, don't you think?'

By far the most ridiculous rivalry I have ever experienced at Haas was the one that existed between Mick Schumacher and Nikita Mazepin. I said earlier that rivalries are usually born when somebody either takes or threatens to take something that another person wants or possesses. Sometimes, though, if the person who wants it doesn't have what it takes, an issue can be created to try and disguise the fact. When genuine rivalries intensify, things like this can often come into play, but when a rivalry is actually based on excuses it isn't good.

When Gene and I launched the Haas F1 Team to an unsuspecting public back in 2016 the sport itself was in a very different place. The hierarchy on the grid, for instance, was much more defined than it is today and there was no F1 Commission (at least as it is today), which is the group that makes many of the strategic decisions concerning the sport and is made up of representatives from all ten teams plus representatives from F1 and the FIA. What you had back then was the F1 Strategy Group, which comprised

FIA and F1 representatives, plus representatives from only Ferrari, Red Bull and Mercedes (or their previous incarnations), McLaren, Williams and the highest-finishing other team in the previous year's Constructors' Championship. As I've said, the other teams such as Haas were allowed to attend the meetings but didn't have a vote, and only ever had a say in anything thanks to an earlier incarnation of the F1 Commission which at the time represented the other interested parties such as the smaller teams and race promoters. It was bullshit, basically, and remained in place until Liberty Media took charge. Had Bernie remained at the helm nothing would have changed. After all, not all of Bernie's friends are fans of democracy.

These days Formula 1 is still a meritocracy, in that if you do better you get more, but at least the F1 Commission in its present form includes representatives from every team on the grid, so is indeed a democracy. In terms of creating competition between the teams and drivers, having things on more of a level playing field has obviously paid dividends and many new rivalries have been created. What's changed, though, is that instead of the vast majority of these rivalries being between the drivers, it's more about the teams. Or should I say, the team principals.

In 2021 the Max Verstappen versus Lewis Hamilton rivalry produced one of the most dramatic moments ever seen in Formula 1, yet it isn't what people remember. Sure, Max and Lewis were driving the cars, but what stays in our memories is Toto Wolff losing his shit with race director Michael Masi, and Christian Horner crying with joy, like a little boy who has been good on Christmas morning. Wherever your allegiance lies, the rivalry between Christian and Toto has been, and still is, a great source of entertainment. It is also completely genuine, believe it or not. Sure, I like taking the piss out of Toto and Christian from time to time (or most of the time), but these guys are at the very top of one of the biggest sports on the planet and their differences in character and personality (not to mention height!), which seem to align exactly with the culture of the teams they represent, make for an almost perfect rivalry and one that I hope will continue making me die laughing for many years to come.

All together now: 'NO MICHAEL, NO MICHAEL, THAT WAS SO NOT RIGHT!'

2023

THE OVERVIEW

After finishing the previous section I was left asking myself whether the 2022 season had lived up to expectations. Not in terms of variety and drama – that season is the GOAT as far as I am concerned – but in terms of results and what we achieved. Having now given it a bit of thought I would say that it probably exceeded expectations. Or at least mine. After 2021 everybody thought that Haas would be in last place for ever. We had been flatlining for two years, and had it not been for Williams we would have been the undisputed whipping boys of the sport. What we managed to achieve in 2022 then, with the resources we had at our disposal, was actually pretty impressive. The biggest frustration, of course, is that with fewer mistakes made by the team, and especially the FIA, it could easily have been better. Such is life.

With hindsight, this is probably the point in time when I should have shaken Gene's hand and walked away from it all. Right from the very start of our relationship our only real ambition had been for the team to keep on progressing no matter what. It is human nature to want to make and do things better and for the first few years I think we achieved that.

There were no objectives set in stone. There was no endgame. The goal was to progress, see where it took us and enjoy the journey.

As important as it is to want to improve something and progress, you also need to know when you are fighting a losing battle. I did, I think, but I failed to do anything about it. In my eyes, Gene no longer had a vision for the team and his relationship with the sport had changed. What had started out as an enjoyable sporting adventure (for both of us) had to him, in my opinion, become an expensive inconvenience. For example, when the team's new title sponsor, MoneyGram International, came on board, Gene was going to buy a new motorhome. The existing one looked like shit and was by far the oldest in the paddock. It looked so out of place. I did all the groundwork getting the quotes together and everything but when it came to signing the cheque Gene changed his mind. 'We'll stick with the one we've got,' he said.

Gene Haas in 2015 would not have acted like that. He would have bought the motorhome and just got on with it. Also, back then the team was worth nothing as a going concern whereas now it was worth anything up to a billion dollars. It made no sense at all and was very frustrating.

His argument was that it didn't make the car go faster. Really? I am a firm believer that better equipment can motivate people, raise standards and set the culture, and in turn could and would have had a material effect on our performance on the track. You see what I mean though. The vision had gone.

The question you must now be asking yourselves is, if all that is true, why the hell did I decide to stay? That's actually quite an easy one. First and foremost, I stayed for the team. At the risk of repeating myself, I had been involved in recruiting almost every member of staff at Haas and many of them had been with us since day one. They were like family to me. Does that sound sentimental? Possibly a bit. It is true though. I felt responsible for them, all of them, which is why I didn't leave. I was like an overbearing father who says too many rude words and embarrasses everybody at parties, whereas Gene was like a mysterious rich uncle who appears every so often out of nowhere but who nobody really knows.

Anyway, who's up for a few pages with a lot of use of the phrase 'tyre degradation'? You are? That disappoints me, because I'm not.

Before we started making headlines for going through tyres like the FIA go through lame excuses, the majority of news the team created just prior to the start of the 2023 season was about our new driver line-up, consisting of Kevin and Nico Hülkenberg. The reason people were getting excited was because in 2017 at the Hungarian Grand Prix they had had a bump on the track that resulted in Nico saying something to Kevin in the press pen afterwards. I think he accused him of not being a very good sportsman or something. Anyway, had it been left there it would all have been forgotten, but this is Kevin Magnussen we're talking about. He's a feisty little bastard! Instead of turning the other cheek and just ignoring Nico he instructed him to do something very rude to his private parts which, because he was being interviewed, was caught on camera. At the time I don't remember it being much of an issue but when the partnership was announced for 2023 it was all of a sudden headline news. Phrases such as 'Bad blood', 'No love lost' and 'We're expecting fireworks' were commonplace in the press and in the end I had to make enquiries.

'Is there anything in this shit, Kevin?' I asked. 'Surely you guys have sorted everything out.'

'We did, about a year ago,' he said. 'We've both grown up a bit since then. We're also fathers now.'

'Thank fok for that,' I said. 'The last thing I need at the start of the season is you and Nico giving each other shit.'

'Don't worry, we're cool.'

By the time we arrived for testing Kevin and Nico had spent quite a bit of time together and my sources confirmed that they had been getting on pretty well. In all seriousness, this was a big relief for me. I had high hopes for the new line-up and did not want any negativity or distractions.

Before we move on, let me tell you what my hopes were going into 2023 – apart from Kevin and Nico not killing each other. One of my hopes was that we would make fewer headlines. Despite our successes, 2022 had been pretty crazy in that regard and I was hoping for a quieter year in comparison. My expectation was that it probably would not turn out like that, but you never know. When it came to our performances on the track the best I could really hope for was some kind of improvement on 2022. As always, we had no idea what the other teams had been doing during the off season which kept everything measured.

Looking back, I think my final hope for 2023 was that the Gene situation might get resolved somehow. While we had not fallen out exactly, by this time we only really spoke to each other when we had to and my frustrations over the lack of investment were starting to bother me. Given the current state of the team versus the current state of the sport – as in, what the other teams were now investing and what might be happening in the future – I could not see us being able to manage ninth in the Championship, let alone fifth or sixth. Sponsorship was healthy but that only helped us to survive day to day, which was how the team had been operating for a long time. There was no long-term plan. No vision. Normally I am not a defeatist, but while Gene had been losing his passion and vision for the team (and had been as early as 2019) I had been losing hope. I'd been in some shit situations in my time but never one like this. Not that I ever considered giving up. That isn't something I am good at.

At Jaguar there had been a thousand and one reasons why things did not work out. It was frustrating for sure, but it was also beyond saving, which made it easier to walk away from. Or, in mine and Niki's case, easier to get pushed out of the door! At Haas it was the polar opposite. For a start, the sport was in a considerably better place than it had been when I was at Jaguar. In fact, apart from the name and the fact that we still raced cars with four wheels and at many of the same circuits, it was almost unrecognizable. Then you had the people. Sure, we had a pretty good team at Jaguar, but due to the evolutionary nature of the sport the guys at Haas were on a different level. Regardless of this, they could only perform to the best of their ability if they had the best resources at their disposal. And then you had the team itself. As well as being worth a billion as a going concern, with a bit of investment I knew Haas could easily get back to being in the midfield again and then fight to become the best of the rest. With even more investment, who knows? I wasn't suggesting throwing money at the team just for the sake of it. What's more, with the budget cap in place you could not do that any more. The fact is, however, that if you are not even prepared to spend what you are allowed to, you put yourself at an immediate disadvantage. That was our situation, and it was becoming a big problem.

THE TEST

This is going to be the shortest chapter in the book, if not the entire world!

Testing went like a foking dream. Understanding the fundamentals of the new car – check. Plenty of laps (415 in total) – check. Qualifying simulations – check. Race simulations – check. Aero testing – check. High fuel runs – check. Testing different tyre compounds – check check check. Nico and Kevin were as happy as pigs in shit by the end of the final day and only got out of the car to visit the toilet. The only issue we noticed that caused any concern was some unexpected tyre degradation that we suffered during longer runs.

We weren't too worried though. It'd be fine.

Ahem.

THE SEASON

Are you sure I cannot talk you into skipping this part of the story? No? Guys, come on. I thought we had a relationship. OK, if I really have to. You asked for it though. I warn you, it is not going to be very pretty. Grown-ups could be crying by the end of this, I hope you know that.

One of the reasons we decided to go with Nico Hülkenberg was because we knew he was quick in qualifying, and he justified that part of our decision immediately with P10 at the first race in Bahrain. Kevin's chances of progressing out of Q1 were scuppered by traffic but he was happy with the car and the early signs were good.

The tyre degradation issue had reared its head again during FP1 but it was only during the race that we started to realize it might be problematic. Nico, who ended up finishing P15 (Kevin finished P13), said afterwards that during the race he had been going through tyres like a hot knife through butter. Kevin, on the other hand, felt like we had made a big step forward since FP1 in that regard so although we were concerned the jury was still out.

Saudi Arabia proved to be the ultimate false dawn. After both cars made it through to Q2 (Nico lined up P11 and Kevin P13) they each had a flawless race with Kevin finishing P10, scoring our first point of the season, and Nico P12. Obviously we would have preferred to score double points, but tyre management hadn't been an issue for either driver so we came away feeling cautiously optimistic. As far as we were concerned, we were well and truly in the mix.

The following race in Australia had everything. Lots of drama, some anger at the end and, fortunately, a few points for Haas. The drama began when Kevin lost a tyre at turn two towards the end of the race which led to a red flag and a standing restart. Carlos Sainz then tapped Fernando Alonso into a spin which sent him and several other cars crashing out. After another red flag the race was restarted under caution during the final lap and the order of classification at the end of the race had Nico P4. That's right guys, I said P4!

Before we had time to celebrate I got word that, for reasons that would take too long to explain here and would send you all to sleep, the stewards had decided to revert to the classification prior to the second restart which put Nico P7. That was still good, of course, but it wasn't P4. We duly lodged a protest (after I got quite angry) which was dismissed and so we had to make do. As importantly, at least in terms of the story I am telling, we came away having experienced little in the way of tyre degradation. The optimism was becoming louder.

In Baku the problem returned for Nico but not for Kevin. The same thing happened again in Miami, where Kevin scored a point. After that, things just turned to shit. Qualifying produced some astonishing results for the team with Nico lining up on the front row of the grid in Canada. He had some luck with a red flag courtesy of Oscar Piastri towards the end of the session, but who cares? Under normal circumstances we would have been jumping around like infected idiots at such news but it was marred by a feeling of inevitability. An inevitability that we would not be able to convert it into points.

As if making sure that we would end the weekend with absolutely fok all, the stewards summonsed Nico after qualifying for a red flag infraction and then dropped him three places. Even starting from the third row of the grid should have been a cause for celebration, but it wasn't. The teams around us, some of which had encountered a similar tyre problem at the start of the season, had all been pushing on and improving whereas we were going backwards. Not literally, I am happy to say, but only just.

The issue, by the way, was being caused by a dramatic forward centre of pressure shift during braking and in the corner entry phase. This can work wonders in getting the front tyres working over one lap in qualifying – and it did – but after time it starts hammering the rear tyres. When that happens, traction occurs and things start going wrong.

The mistake I made at this point in the season was to continue to try and rectify the issue in the wind tunnel, when what I should have done, and eventually did, was to look elsewhere and in doing so free up the wind tunnel time for the development of next season's car. There comes a point in time when you have to draw a line under things and I fully admit that in this instance I was late on that. Gene was getting more and more pissed with the results and instead of just taking it on the chin like I usually did when he started moaning I became obsessed with trying to shut him up. That's the truth of it.

When we eventually made the decision to stop developing the VF-23 in the wind tunnel, the guys in Maranello were free to begin developing the VF-24. They still had enough time, so they said, so it was all good. Well, 'good' is probably stretching the truth a little bit, but you know what I mean. It's ironic, but as part of that development they would still have to try and get to grips with the tyre degradation issue. They'd just be doing it on a new car.

The last four races of the season went pretty much the same in terms of results, which consolidated our position at the bottom of the Constructors' Championship. A lot was then made about Haas having finished either ninth or tenth in four of the last five seasons, but without any mention at all of Covid or the fact that we were forced to run with an undeveloped car. A year earlier that would not have bothered me one little bit, but now I'd had enough.

Regardless of how a season had gone, I would always be full of hope after the final race and my mind would start filling with thoughts about how we could improve and what we might be able to achieve the following year. I promise you, as much as I like spending time with my family I could not wait for things to start up again. Not now though. When Kevin took the chequered flag in last position in Abu Dhabi I felt despondent. The determination I spoke of a little bit earlier had disappeared. Not that I let it show. I always claim that I am not a good actor, but perhaps I have got that wrong. I obviously wasn't swinging from the chandeliers when the season came to an end, but at the same time I did not have my head in my hands. Inside, though, I was feeling pretty numb.

PIT STOP

THE FIA

This is going to be fun.

The difference between the FIA circa 2014 when we got the licence and the FIA today would make a book in itself. Even so, it isn't one that I would particularly want to read or help to write. My differences of opinion with the current president, Mohammed Ben Sulayem, for instance, have become pretty well known over the past couple of years, and comparing him with Jean Todt, who in my opinion was an excellent president, is like comparing apples with pears. Don't get me wrong, Mohammed's a nice guy, but his era in charge has been chaotic so far and he's managed to upset just about every team and every team principal. Jean, on the other hand, always ran a steady ship and managed to get on with just about everybody. Unlike Mohammed, he had a background in F1 and that inspired confidence.

The person the FIA, not to mention the sport of Formula 1 in general, misses most of all is Charlie Whiting. From a personal point of view, not only was Charlie a good friend of mine but he gave me a huge amount of advice when we started Haas and without him things would have been different for us. In fact, without Charlie's help there's a chance we might not have made it on to the grid.

A few years later, in 2018, Charlie came to our rescue once again by publicly refuting the claims made by some idiots that the sharing of technology between Haas and Ferrari was against the rules. Haas had made a flying start to the 2018 season and so one or two people who weren't doing quite as well started moaning. 'We know exactly what's going on between Haas and Ferrari,' said Charlie, 'which is completely legal. We've not seen anything that concerns us.' Had anybody else come out and said that, although it would have been welcome it wouldn't have had any effect on the rumour mill. Not with Charlie. They were his rules and his regulations and that was the end of it. He had written many of them so you never doubted his interpretation. Above all, though, he had the respect of everybody involved in the sport – the drivers, the mechanics, the team principals, the engineers. Everybody who had any experience of working in Formula 1 respected and, more often than not, liked Charlie Whiting. In fact, I cannot think of a more credible person who has worked in the sport.

Because of the respect you always had for the likes of Charlie and Jean, and because they respected you, if you ever had an argument with them, which was inevitable, it would be forgotten about within a few minutes. That was just the way of it. We were all mature human beings and each one would take on board what the other said. Sometimes we'd agree and sometimes we'd agree to disagree. The point is, we always ended up shaking hands and moving on.

In 2017 I had a disagreement with Charlie about permanent race stewards that ended up going public. Due to the number of controversial decisions that were being made, which often affected the smaller teams more than they did the bigger teams, I wanted F1 to put in place a panel of stewards who knew their stuff and who would attend every race on the calendar. I put the idea to Charlie and over the space of a few weeks we had several meetings about it. After giving it some consideration he came to the conclusion that, in his opinion, a permanent panel would result in more questions than answers. 'The way we do things at the moment is more reasonable in my opinion,' said Charlie. 'So it's a no. Sorry, Guenther.' I must admit to being a bit pissed with the decision, but I respected it.

These days, if you have a disagreement with the FIA there often have to be consequences, and it perhaps won't surprise you to learn that I only received my first official reprimand from the FIA after Charlie passed away. It was late September 2019, during the Russian Grand Prix (it had to be the foking Russian one!). I made a comment about a steward over the team radio. I made it after the steward in question issued Kevin Magnussen with a five-second time penalty for rejoining the track after going off at turn two. My exact words were, 'If we didn't have a stupid idiotic steward we would be eighth . . . You know who is the steward. You know him.

It is always the same. He just does not get any more intelligent . . .' The message was broadcast to the public and was later carried by a number of media outlets. Good coverage then!

After being hauled in front of the panel I was fined €7,500 and told not to do it again. I didn't have any problem with the fine, by the way. They have a code of conduct and I broke it. What I did have a problem with was the fact that the steward in question, who in my opinion had a shocking record, was free to carry on making these mistakes without any comeback. It wasn't even a consideration that they might have been in the wrong. While Charlie would still have fined me, and rightly so, he would also have listened to my side of the story, which would have helped me to retain confidence in the governing body. That isn't what happened though. In my opinion the FIA post-Charlie Whiting have ceased being culpable for their mistakes and have lost their humility. That isn't a good situation.

Look at the Max versus Lewis spectacle in Abu Dhabi at the end of the 2021 season. Wherever your loyalties lie with that one (and yes, I agree, it was amazing entertainment), from a regulations point of view it was a shit show of biblical proportions, and regardless of what decision Charlie Whiting might have made in Michael Masi's position there would have been far less controversy and embarrassment. Oh, fok it. We all know what Charlie would have done. Had he been at the helm Lewis would now be an eight-time world champion.

When I started writing this bit I Googled my name and the FIA, and in 0.32 seconds it delivered 307,000 results. Not all of them will be about arguments or reprimands, but a fair amount will. Regardless of which, I think I should tell you about my final 'experiences' with the organization and then move on. Otherwise this will just end up being a long list of fines and complaints. Another time, maybe. Or maybe not.

The last time I was reprimanded by the FIA was in June 2023. It was a steward-related incident (surprise, surprise) that happened after a collision involving Nico Hülkenberg during the Monaco Grand Prix and had me calling once again for a permanent panel. I ended up referring to stewards as 'laymen', which they didn't take kindly to.

'Every professional sport,' I said in the offending interview, 'has got professionals being referees and stuff like this. F1 is one of the biggest sports in the world and we still have laymen deciding on the fate of people that invest millions in their careers. It's always a discussion because there's no consistency. I don't want to blame any particular person on this, but if they're not all there all the time [a permanent panel] then this is just like any other job. In fact, it's not even a job because in a job you can get sacked, because you get paid, and if you do a bad job you get sacked. You cannot get sacked because you do not get paid. I think we need to step it up.'

The issue came about because we each had a different interpretation of the word 'laymen'. My interpretation referred to people who worked in a certain job only occasionally, which was correct and had always been my main issue when it came to stewards. Whereas their interpretation of a layman was somebody who lacked qualifications. Either way, they thought I was being disrespectful and I had to apologize. It was a misunderstanding, that's all. Looking back, the vast majority of my run-ins with the FIA have been either about or related to my strong belief that a permanent panel of stewards is necessary and will benefit the sport immeasurably, and I believe that to this day.

Funnily enough, my swansong with the FIA came about both during and after Haas's home Grand Prix in 2023 at the Circuit of the Americas. Although it was arduous, costly and a complete pain in the foking ass, it resulted in a little victory that, you never know, might one day result in change.

As I'm sure you'll appreciate, given what happened during the 2023 season, there are few phrases in the sport that affect me more adversely than 'tyre degradation'. In fact, the only one that comes close is 'track limits'. Jeezoz Christ, where do I foking start with this one?

If memory serves me correctly the problem happened at turn six. A load of cars had been exceeding track limits there on multiple occasions but because the FIA didn't have cameras in place they were never penalized. While I was definitely in agreement that the variable targeted approach from Charlie's era, where only certain corners on certain circuits were focused on, needed updating, the fact that the

FIA were unable to police this properly had left them wide open and it was becoming a foking joke. 'If certain corners on certain tracks require properly angled CCTV cameras for track limits,' I said in an interview, 'surely it is a basic requirement that the required number of cameras should be in place before each race.' They weren't, and on this occasion Haas ended up losing out.

After gathering and then studying the footage that *was* available, which in our view proved conclusively that Checo, Lance Stroll, Alex Albon and Logan Sargeant had all committed multiple offences during the race (in Logan's case a five-second penalty would have put Nico Hülkenberg into tenth position, thus winning him a point), we decided to submit a right of review request that we hoped would trigger a review.

After two meetings with the FIA involving the respective team managers, part of whose job is to liaise with the FIA, the right to review request was rejected on the grounds that the evidence we presented had already been available at the time of the original stewards' decisions on Sunday night. Far more importantly, this evidence had not been considered sufficient due to the lack of fixed CCTV footage.

The victory I mentioned came in a press release that was made by the stewards afterwards. They said:

> Our inability to properly enforce the current standard for track limits for all competitors is completely

unsatisfactory and therefore we strongly recommend to all concerned that a solution to prevent further reoccurrences of this widespread problem be rapidly deployed. Whether the problem is properly addressed by better technology solutions, track modifications, a combination thereof, or a different regulation and enforcement standard, the stewards leave to those better positioned to make such assessments.

Of course, I had to have my say after that.

'They should make sure that they've got the means in place to check their own regulations, not me sitting at home or Aston Martin [who protested over a similar matter in Austria] checking what they are doing. That is not the team's job. In half an hour, we didn't have time to go through all that stuff because that is not our job. We are not the governing body, we are a race team, we pay somebody to do this job – the FIA.'

Halle-foking-lujah!

DECEMBER 2023

HAASTA LA VISTA, BABY

If I had ever had to take a guess at where I would find out that my time running the team I had dreamed up, later formed and then dedicated over ten years of my life to had come to an end, a supermarket in Merano in northern Italy would not even have been in my top five. But what would your top five have been, Guenther? I hear you ask. On the toilet would have to be number one. And number two, of course. Number three would be in the car, which is where I spent quite a bit of my time when I was not at home or at a race track. Number four the office, or one of them, which is probably where I used to spend the majority of my waking hours, and number five in bed. There you are.

A supermarket in Merano was where it happened though. It was Friday 29 December 2023, in the afternoon, and I was standing at the deli counter staring at a nice-looking piece of ham when all of a sudden my phone started ringing. Who the foking hell's this? I remember thinking. It was Gene. He'd been trying to get hold of me for a day or two but because of the time difference between Italy and California we'd missed each other. I didn't even think about what he might want.

'Hi Gene,' I said. 'How are you? Happy Christmas.'

I'm not usually keen on answering telephone calls when I'm

in the process of trying to choose quality pork-based products in an Italian supermarket at Christmas time, but at the end of the day he was my boss.

'I'm fine,' he said. 'Happy Christmas to you too.' He then spent a minute or so talking about not very much at all, and I was just about to ask him where all this was leading when he stopped and changed the subject. Thank God. 'Why do you think we've been doing so badly, Guenther?' he asked.

'We've been through this a million times, Gene,' I said. 'In order for us to improve you have to invest some money and get us closer to the budget cap.'

There then followed a mini tirade about how much money he had invested in the team over the years, which I countered by reminding him that the team had recently been valued at close to a billion dollars, and that I had even recently found him $200 million in external investment, which he had declined. 'I also know some people who are interested in buying the team outright, Gene,' I said. 'Just say the word.' Another mini tirade followed about him not wanting to sell the team, which I had been expecting, and then he stopped.

'Anyway, Guenther, your contract is up for renewal and I've decided not to renew it.'

'OK, Gene, that's fine with me,' I said, and then I hung up.

The call cannot have lasted more than six or seven minutes front to back. After ten years.

Given what had happened over the season and our impasse regarding investment and the budget cap, I maybe should have been expecting it. The fact is, however, that by the end of 2023 I was numb and had not been able to consider anything very much at all, apart from how the hell we were going to get out of the mess we were in. All of a sudden, the feelings of inertia that had consumed me for as long as I could remember lifted. I was a free man.

'Who was that?' Gertie asked casually. She had absolutely no idea what had just happened.

'That was Gene,' I said. 'He's let me go.'

'He's what?!' Her voice must have gone up at least an octave and doubled in volume.

'He's let me go,' I repeated. 'As of now, I am no longer the team principal of the Haas F1 Team. I am a late-middle-aged unemployed man.'

'But he can't do that.'

'He can, and he has. It's his team. Guess what this means though? I'm a free man, Gertie.'

For the next couple of minutes we just stood there at the deli counter in the supermarket trying to take it all in. As I said, perhaps I should have been expecting it, but I wasn't. Then again, I don't remember feeling shocked at all. Perhaps if we had been doing well at the time I would have been (I'd probably have been furious!), but it all seemed OK. I'm a pretty philosophical guy when it comes to things like this and I still had my family, my health — which would probably improve quite a bit now — and my friends. I also had a half-share in a very successful company, a flourishing career as an author of quality high-end literature with mass-market appeal, a two-year-old Toyota Tundra and a new dog that Greta had been asking for. Where the fok did it all go wrong, Guenther?

What I also *didn't* have any more was the responsibility of running a Formula 1 team that employed over two hundred people and having to explain to the world and his wife every day of the week why we had been doing so badly without telling them the truth and going into detail about my ongoing battle with Gene over investment. While I appreciate the value of not letting a little thing like the truth get in the way of a good story, having to hide the truth over a prolonged period of time and from people who are not stupid can be downright problematic. I was absolutely fed up with having to bullshit people, but now, at long last, it was at an end.

'Shall we go home?' I said to Gertie eventually. 'I need to have a sit down and a think about things.'

'Of course, let's go.'

By the time we arrived home about twenty minutes later my mind, which for as long as I can remember has had a default position of 'glass is half full', had gone into overdrive. In addition to feeling like I'd had the weight of the world lifted from my shoulders, I was excited about what lay ahead of me. You know what they say, when one door closes two doors open, and the more I thought about it the more excited and animated I became.

'Are you sure you're OK with this, Guenther?' Gertie asked me later that evening. 'Haas has been your life for ten years. It's a lot to take in.'

'I don't deny that Haas has been a big part of my life,' I said, 'but at the same time, nothing lasts for ever. As I said in the supermarket, I'm free now. Free to be a father to Greta and a husband to you. I've just realized: because I'm unemployed, that makes me a house husband and a stay-at-home dad! How crazy is that?'

I cannot say for sure what went through Gertie's mind as I said those words but she looked pretty alarmed. We'd been married for almost thirty years but in all that time I'd spent between a third and a half of every year away from home. Now, poor Gertie was faced with the prospect of having her excitable and irritating husband at home for the majority of the time.

'Greta will be thrilled,' she said eventually.

'I hope so. When do you think we should tell her?'

'On the plane home,' said Gertie.

'Nowhere for her to run when she starts screaming, you mean?'

'GUENTHER!'

'Sorry.'

The reason Gertie suggested delaying telling Greta for a couple of days was because she wasn't sure how she would react. Not to the news that her father was going to be able to spend more time with her at last, but to the news that I was no longer running Haas. 'You know what kids are like,' said Gertie. 'Because you're well known she might be worried about a backlash or about having to answer lots of questions from people.'

Just as Gertie suspected, when we finally got round to breaking the news to Greta during the flight home her reaction was a mixture of happiness, thank God that the 'old man', as she now calls me, was going to be around a lot more from now on, and a little bit of apprehension about what her schoolfriends might say. Within a day or two, though, the apprehension had lifted so everyone was happy. Gertie knew full well that I wasn't going to be at home every day of the year (if I was, she might have applied for my old job!) and we all had a lot to look forward to.

'I haven't seen you like this in years,' said Gertie the morning after we arrived home in North Carolina.

'Like what?'

'You have a spring in your step, like you used to have.'

I thought about this for a while and came to the conclusion that the 'spring in my step', as Gertie put it, had probably started disappearing in 2020, which is when Covid and all the other issues started landing and when the lack of investment in the team began having a material effect. Prior to that, despite the odd hiccup here and there, we had four years when we got more things right than we got wrong and were a competitive team that people both inside and outside the sport respected and took seriously. Given some of the bullshit that has been written about the team over the years that's hard to believe, but it's true.

This is a pretty bold statement, but I would say that one of the main things that kept us afloat in the years after 2020, which is when I basically swapped running a competitive motor racing team for mainly problem-solving and firefighting, in terms of both team morale and exposure, was *Drive to Survive*. Had that not come along Haas would not have had the love that people have shown the team over recent years, and I know for a fact that it made a big difference. The team had problems both on and off the track but the general public wanted us to do well. It was no substitute for being competitive on the track, of course, but it made it much easier to keep on fighting.

I'm trying to think of what questions you might like answering before I sign off. I suppose one of the obvious ones would be, if I had my time again, would I do anything different? The answer is yes, I would. Bearing in mind what has happened, if I had my time again I would try to find more outside investment prior to setting up the team as opposed to leaving everything to one man and one wallet. Gene obviously had his reasons why he stopped investing in the team but that does not change the fact that it ended up having a detrimental effect on performance and was, in my opinion, the primary reason why the team had struggled over recent years. Did I get everything right? No, of course I didn't. Despite what you might think I am a human being and all human beings are fallible. I tried my best always, and that is all that anyone can ever do.

What I have just said has nothing to do with sour grapes, by the way. Come on, you know that isn't my style. The fact is that had I told the press what was happening, Gene and I would have fallen out publicly which would have been damaging to the team. Also, until quite recently I always held out hope that perhaps one day he would change his mind and start investing again. Perhaps I should have called him out publicly as it might have instigated change. Foking hindsight. It gets on my nerves sometimes.

I suppose the most relevant question that I can address here is what might I do next professionally. After all, I cannot stay unemployed for ever. In reality, as I write this it has only been a few months since I was let go, but you know what I mean. And I've never been busier, which is kind of ironic. In fact, the last time I received so many calls, emails and messages was just after Russia invaded Ukraine and Haas became sporting enemy number one. On that occasion I was under strict instructions from Stuart Morrison not to speak to anybody, and for once in my life I did exactly as I was told. I remember turning my phone off to start with and then every half an hour or so I'd turn it on again for a minute to see what was happening. What can I say, I'm curious! Each time I did it there were dozens of missed calls and God knows how many messages and emails. It was quite overwhelming, despite the fact that I ignored most of them. When Haas released the statement about them not renewing my contract the same thing happened again, except this time the vast majority of people wanted to wish me well, which is nice. They also wanted to know what had gone on, of course, but I guess they're also entitled to be curious. 'You'll have to buy the book,' I said to them.

In among all the well-wishers were a few people I knew who wanted to talk to me about future opportunities, and if I were a betting man, which fortunately I am not, I would put a few lira on one or two of them coming off. One thing's for sure, I'm certainly not going to be turning into a recluse and growing a beard any time soon. If there's one thing I have learned about myself over the last ten years it's that first and foremost I am a people person. This was first suggested to me about two and a half years ago during a meeting with my publishers about *Surviving to Drive*. I remember one of them said something like, 'We want to find out what makes Guenther Steiner tick.'

'Nothing makes me tick,' I said. 'I'm not a foking clock. I'm just a normal guy.'

They had no answer to that.

We went round in circles like this for about twenty minutes until one of the people in the meeting suggested that I was very much a people person.

'Am I?' I asked.

'I think you are.'

The other people in the meeting seemed to agree with this

idea so I decided to go away and think about it. And guess what, they were right. Everything I have achieved in my life professionally, from landing a cushy job as a chauffeur for a General during my national service to starting my own business before selling the idea of starting a Formula 1 team to Gene and then getting a licence from Bernie and the FIA, has been achieved not because I am super intelligent or anything, but because I am a people person. I also have to know my shit, of course, and have a lot of endeavour and ideas. But had I not been able to communicate these and get on with the people concerned I would not even have got past first base. That's my only real talent, I think: an ability to get on with and relate to a lot of different people. And deliver bad news, of course. The former is not a bad one to have though, don't you think?

What makes it enjoyable is that I am naturally quite a sociable person and people genuinely interest me. I don't always take to everyone I meet (who the hell does?), but I can usually find some common ground if I have to and it's very rare that I fall out with anyone. That only usually happens with people I know well, and often has more to do with clearing the air than anything else. A bit of honesty and a few well-chosen swear words are sometimes just what a relationship needs.

My greatest triumph in this regard is probably getting the licence for Haas, for the simple reason that I had to convince a room full of very powerful but unique people, who all had different opinions and ideas, that what we were proposing was financially viable and would be good for the sport. We're back to betting again, but had a bookmaker offered odds before the meeting started on us getting the licence they would have been similar to the odds you would have got for Haas winning the World Championship with Mick and Nikita in 2021. Nobody in the world thought we stood a chance of getting that licence, except for me.

Looking back, although my presentation of the proposal went well, in that nobody fell into a coma or left the room, what got me the meeting in the first place was that a relationship already existed between me and most of the people there. I'm not saying that we were all the best of friends, but over the years I had got to know them pretty well and so no introductions were necessary.

Incidentally, just because you are involved in a sport or a business for a long time does not mean that you will automatically get to know everyone who is involved. You have to make an effort, and once again that is something I enjoy. Not everybody is happy to see me though. Over the years there have been people who would run and hide if they saw me approaching them in the paddock. Not because they are scared of me. At least, I don't think they are. I'm just not their kind of person. I tend not to take these things too seriously. I have an opinion about lots of people in the paddock but they would have to have done something pretty bad to stop me from saying hello or having a chat with them. Life's too short for that kind of bullshit.

Ever since joining Jaguar in 2001 I'd had ambitions to move up in the sport, and in order to do that, and to do my job at Jaguar properly, I had to knock on a lot of doors, shake a lot of hands and get to know a lot of people. And I mean, get to know them. It's no good just saying hello to somebody, making some small talk and then handing them a business card. That's just networking. What I set out to do with the likes of Bernie Ecclestone, Charlie Whiting and Jean Todt was try and form some kind of relationship with them, partly because it was obviously relevant to my professional responsibilities and ambitions, but also because I am an inquisitive human being who enjoys meeting other human beings. Seriously, who in motorsport would not want to get to know the likes of Charlie and Bernie? Lastly, I figured that by getting to know the likes of Bernie, Charlie and Jean, who were right at the top of the tree and whose combined experience in motorsport came to about six hundred years, I might also learn a thing or two. No shit, Sherlock.

As you know, the guy who got me into F1 in the first place was Niki Lauda, and the reason he first asked to see me all those years ago was because he'd heard from some friends of his in the rally industry – people who I had made an effort to get to know and form a relationship with – that I got things done, had some good ideas occasionally and was loyal and reliable. Going for the licence was like history repeating itself, both in terms of the opportunity that presented itself, which again was pretty special, and the fact that it was down to who I knew as much as what I knew.

The other area of my life where my 'talent' has come in handy is *Drive to Survive*. Or should I say, the aftermath of me appearing on *Drive to Survive*. Bearing in mind what has happened since then, if I didn't enjoy meeting new people I would have thrown away my phone and gone to live on an island somewhere. Before it all exploded the vast majority of my time was spent either with my family at home or with the guys at Haas and in F1. That was still a lot of people though. At least a few hundred. Then, post-March 2019, that number went up slightly, and not just in terms of people who had been watching *Drive to Survive*. You had the press and the media, who were a lot more interested in me now than they used to be. The reason why the transition from me being a well-known fish in a small pond to a well-known fish in a foking ginormous pond has been so smooth is because, just like the guys at the publishers suggested, I am a people person. Do you know what? As a label I am completely OK with that.

Actually, there is one more question that I think needs answering here and that is what I intend to do with all this newfound free time. According to Gertie, I have been on a permanent holiday since 1986, which is slightly unfair. In truth, because of the amount of travelling I have been doing we have never really done holidays. Or at least not in the traditional way, such as going skiing or flying to a hot country for two weeks and sitting by a pool. I cannot imagine sitting by a pool for two hours, let alone two weeks. I'd be bored out of my mind! Fortunately, so would Gertie and Greta, so what we tended to do while I was with Haas was have a few days away here and there. Sometimes we'd mix it in with a race weekend, so they'd come to wherever I was in the world on the Friday and we'd stay until the Tuesday, or we'd do it during a break in the F1 calendar. It was sensible to make use of my nomadic lifestyle.

Take Vegas, for instance. The whole world was excited about Formula 1 visiting Las Vegas in 2023, including Greta and Gertie. 'Then why don't you come over and watch the race?' I suggested. They didn't need asking twice. Because we were all so used to it, I didn't need to explain to Greta and Gertie that despite them being in Vegas for the race I would not be able to spend much time with them on the Friday and Saturday. Conversely, they did not need to explain to me that they were absolutely fine with that. While I was working they would go shopping and sightseeing and then at mealtimes we would all get together. Vegas was slightly different, though, as the number of events I had to attend was off the scale. Fortunately, these were mainly social events so Gertie and Greta were happy to come along with me. A good time was had by all in the end, I think. Even Max Verstappen.

What I think will end up happening now is just more of the same, and to be honest with you, I cannot wait. If you include my two seasons with Jaguar and the time I spent putting Haas together I have spent thirteen years travelling hundreds of thousands of miles but seeing almost nothing. A friend of mine from England came to the Singapore Grand Prix in 2023 and saw more of Singapore in three days than I have in a decade. 'The Botanical Gardens are very impressive,' he said on the Friday evening during dinner after I had been at the track all day. 'Especially the orchid garden. You should go and see them. Oh, sorry, you can't, can you. What a shame.'

'Fok off!'

I'm pretty sure I paid for dinner that night too. What a mug.

To make matters worse, the same guy came to Brazil for the Grand Prix in November. 'São Paulo's great for restaurants,' he remarked during what was probably another free foking meal. The fact that he had sampled more of what these places have to offer in a few hours than I had in ten years made me want to change things, and I will.

There's one more thing I haven't mentioned yet about what I'll be doing in the future, and it may come as something of a surprise. About five years ago I was in Merano and the man who had sold me the apartment where we live when we are there talked me into buying a house he had just renovated. What made me say yes to this I have absolutely no idea but that's exactly what I did.

'You've done what?' said Gertie.

'I've bought a five-bedroom house in the centre of Merano.'

'But why?'

'I don't know why.'

'You don't know why? Oh, Guenther!'

Believe it or not, I am usually very well behaved when it comes to being a husband and I am normally quite communicative. I also don't do things on a whim. What the fok happened?

Once things had calmed down a bit Gertie and I had a sensible conversation about what we were going to do with the house in Merano, and the most viable option seemed to be turning it into a small hotel or a guest house.

'You're going to become a hotelier?' said Stuart Morrison when I told him.

'I know what you're thinking,' I said. 'Don't say another word. You think I'm going to become some kind of Basil foking Fawlty.'

'Actually, that's exactly what I was thinking.'

'I knew it.'

'Who'd be Manuel?'

'I don't know. How about Alonso?'

After a lot of discussions with Gertie, who had as much desire to become a Sybil Fawlty as I did to become Basil, we decided to go with a guest house instead.

'Why don't we have a theme?' Gertie suggested.

'Like what?'

'Like Formula 1.'

'What, you mean have tables made from tyres and name the rooms after drivers or something?'

'No! I mean each suite could be designed with a famous Formula 1 location in mind, such as Singapore or Monte Carlo.'

'No tyres then?'

'No tyres.'

And so, that is exactly what we did. Over the next two years, with the help of an interior designer, Gertie designed five suites that are based on five different locations – Melbourne, Singapore, Suzuka, Monte Carlo and Silverstone. The guest house is called Villa Steiner, and we're both really proud of it. There is still a tiny part of me that wishes we had turned it into a hotel with me hitting Alonso over the head with a frying pan every two minutes and calling the guests wankers, but there we go. You cannot have everything in life.

OK, mis amigos, I'm afraid that our time together is almost at an end. It's been fun though, don't you think? I hope you do. I have definitely enjoyed it. It's a good story. A story that would be hard to make up. Be honest with me, if you were the commissioning editor at a publishing house or a producer at a film studio and a proposal telling this story landed on your desk, what would you do? Call the foking cops, probably. I wonder what's next though. One day I suppose I'll write an autobiography, if anyone's interested, but that won't be for a while. I've still got some living to do. And who knows, one day you might see me back in the paddock – not holding a microphone.

OK, you bunch of rock stars. I'll see you on the other side, wherever that might be.

Ciao.

ACKNOWLEDGEMENTS

Bearing in mind the amount of people who were involved in helping me put Haas F1 together and have kept it moving for so long, not to mention the guys who helped me write and publish such a fine piece of quality literature, this could turn into another foking chapter if I'm not careful! They're worth the paper though. All of them. Before we go on though, if I forget anybody, and I will, I would genuinely like to apologize.

If we're doing this chronologically, which seems sensible, I would first like to thank Chase Carey, Stefano Domenicali, Bernie Ecclestone and the late and eternally great Charlie Whiting and Niki Lauda. You know by now that without these guys I wouldn't have succeeded in making my dream a reality and I will always be in their debt. Not financially though, OK Bernie.

Next, I would like to thank every single person who I hired and/or worked with at Haas F1, from Alan, Pete, Dave-o, Stuart, Kate, Nigel and the rest of the guys who were there from the very beginning, to the people who were employed by the team when I was liberated. You will never know how proud I am of every single one of you and, contrary to popular belief because of what has happened since I left, I would like nothing more than to see the team that I put together with Gene's help succeed, progress and thrive. It's no more than any of you deserve and I wish you all the best.

OK, now we are on to the book. Once again, my partner in crime in what you have just read is a short-arse guy from Leeds who I have now been working with almost constantly for over two years, James Hogg. Thank you Hoggy. If they ask us for a third book, go and buy us a foking air fryer!

I would also like to thank my literary agent, Tim Bates from Peters Fraser + Dunlop, and my publisher, Henry Vines from Penguin Random House. These two posh boys from London are willing to slum it with dropouts like me and Hoggy, and to be honest we make a pretty good team. Onwards and upwards!

Last but by no means least, I would like to thank Gertie and Greta. The support you gave me while I was forming and then running Haas F1 was always unconditional, and I could not have done it without you.

Actually, there are some more people I would like to acknowledge before I go, and those are the F1 fans. Ever since I unwittingly became, and I quote, 'the breakout star of the hit Netflix series *Drive to Survive*', I have received a constant stream of smiles, compliments, handshakes, hugs and good wishes. What more could an old man with a talent for saying the wrong thing at the right time wish for? You make life fun, and I think you're all foking amazing.

PICTURE ACKNOWLEDGEMENTS

Every effort has been made to contact and acknowledge copyright holders, but the publishers apologize for any errors or omissions in this respect and invite corrections for future editions.

Page 1: The author with Niki Lauda at the Brazilian Grand Prix, 2002 © Mark Thompson/Getty Images; with Christian Horner, 2005 © Motorsport/LAT Images; on the phone, 2005 © Motorsport/Sutton Images.

Page 2: Team principals' press conference, Singapore, 2016 © Mark Thompson/Getty Images; testing in Barcelona, 2016 © Motorsport/Sutton Images; celebrating the team's first points, 2016 © Sam Bloxham/Motorsport/LAT Images.

Page 3: The author at the Chinese Grand Prix, 2017 © Motorsport/LAT Images; the walking stick, 2017 © Motorsport/Sutton Images; with Ayao Komatsu and Arron Melvin, 2019 © Charles Coates/Getty Images.

Page 4: The author with Toto Wolff in Austria, 2018 © Pixathlon/Shutterstock; at a press conference, 2020 © Pixathlon/Shutterstock.

PICTURE ACKNOWLEDGEMENTS

Page 5: Romain Grosjean crashes in Bahrain, 2020 © Andy Hone/Motorsport/LAT Images; the author with Grosjean, 2020 © Peter Fox/Getty Images; Covid hits Formula 1, 2022 © Clive Mason/Getty Images.

Page 6: The author with Eddie Irvine in 2022 © Peter Fox/Getty Images; Australian fans, 2022 © Andy Hone/Motorsport/LAT Images; taking photos, 2024 © Clive Mason/Getty Images.

Page 7: *Surviving to Drive* in the wild © Motorsport/LAT Images; the author with Mohammed Ben Sulayem, 2022 © Julien Delfosse/Shutterstock; heading to Downing Street, 2023 © Dan Kitwood/Getty Images.

Page 8: The author in Australia, 2023 © Dan Istitene/Getty Images; in Suzuka, 2023 © Michael Potts/Shutterstock; with Gertie at the Autosport Awards, 2019 © Glenn Dunbar/Motorsport/LAT Images.

ABOUT THE AUTHOR

Guenther Steiner is a motorsport team manager and former mechanic hailing from Merano in northern Italy. From 2014 to the end of 2023 he was the team principal of the Haas F1 Team, having previously been managing director of Jaguar Racing and technical operations director of its subsequent incarnation, Red Bull Racing. In 2014, Guenther persuaded Gene Haas, owner of Haas Automation and NASCAR championship winning team Stewart-Haas Racing, to enter Formula 1.

With their entry in the 2016 season, Haas became the first American constructor to compete in F1 in thirty years. The team took eight points at the 2016 Australian Grand Prix with a sixth-place finish, becoming the first American entry, and the first constructor overall since Toyota Racing in 2002, to score in their debut race. Steiner is also a prominent figure in the cast of the successful Netflix series *Drive to Survive*.